HOLIDAY HILARITY

A HUMOROUS HISTORY
OF CELEBRATION

Jeffrey Gurian
&
Otakara Klettke

DEDICATION

Holidays are supposed to be a joyous time, but for some people, they present great emotional difficulties. This book is dedicated to all those who face any of the holidays with some degree of sadness related to the loss of something or someone dear to them.

On a very personal note, Otakara suffered a terrible tragedy at Christmas time when her mom was hit by a car in the Czech Republic and later passed away due to the injuries.

This event was truly the inspiration for us doing this book.

Jeffrey thinks of his own Mom, Marjorie Gurian very often, but especially around Valentine's Day because her birthday was February 12th.

We wrote this book hoping that we could add a little bit of a humorous perspective to each celebration while honoring those who are no longer here to celebrate with us. Sometimes humor helps us deal with the pain.

XOXOX

Jeffrey and Otakara

TABLE OF CONTENTS

INTRODUCTION

Holidays can be fun, or they can make you want to hang yourself from the nearest Christmas tree. The word "holiday" itself comes from the Old English word "haligdaeg", "halig" meaning "holy" and "daeg" meaning "day." Originally it referred only to special religious days, but it has come to be used to refer to any special day where we choose to rest and not go to school or work.

Some holidays are local, some are national, and a few are even international like Christmas, Chanukah, Easter and major religious holidays. There's a very good chance that America may have the most holidays of any country in the world.

People tend to love holidays because most people tend not to love to go to work or school. We go to school and work mostly because we have to. So we jump at the chance to celebrate any holiday at all, whether it's officially our group's holiday or not, and that's the best example, but a weird way of achieving inclusivity. We're willing to celebrate the holidays of other cultures just to get some time off!

It seems like everyone is willing to do that. Even if the holiday celebrates another religion or culture, as long as they can stay home and get paid for it, people are more than willing to join in.

But anytime there is an upside, unfortunately there is also always a downside. Holidays are extremely stressful for many people. The socially forced "happiness" that may appear as a smile on the outside often masks dark, lonely moments on the inside. December is so stressful to people that January 1st is literally the deadliest day of the year with more people leaving this plane of existence from seemingly natural causes, than on any other day.

In the United States, the main holiday season gets started around the end of the month of November with what we call "Thanksgiving." Thanksgiving, believe it or not, is a national holiday celebrated in Canada, The United States, some of the Caribbean Islands, and get this…, Liberia! Bet you didn't know that!!!

As an example of what we do in this book, the very first Thanksgiving was celebrated in October of 1621, and although neither I nor Otakara were there, according to some historical writings it was supposedly attended by 53 pilgrims and 90 Native Americans to celebrate the first harvest in the New World, which was only the New World to the pilgrims. To the Native Americans it was the only world they had ever known.

The original feast lasted three days, and it became a legal federal holiday in 1863 during the American Civil War, when people from the Northern part of the country and people from the Southern part of the country actually fought and killed each other, and our 16th President, Abraham Lincoln proved it's not always safe to go to the theatre, even if you're wearing a very tall hat, (especially if it's not bulletproof)! It was he who proclaimed a national day of "Thanksgiving" to be celebrated on the fourth Thursday of every November.

But I digress! We'll get back to Thanksgiving later on when we reach November! Thanksgiving in the United States sets the tone for what's coming in December, which are the big religious holidays of Christmas, and Chanukah, leading into New Year's Eve, and assuming you've survived all that, ending on New Year's Day.

This book will take you to visit not all, but many of the

holidays that cause the most stress, and give you some tips on how to handle them without losing your mind, and running at full speed with your head into a wall.

It will also give you some interesting facts about each holiday that you may not have known, plus the history of the holiday, and how it came to be celebrated not only in this country, but sometimes all over the world.

With Otakara living in Oregon and Jeffrey living in New York City we thought we could bring you a diversity of experience.

As I said, our intentions are to bring you a humorous look at the holidays. We want to bring more joy to those who already love holidays, but also to bring a smile to the faces of those who struggle during the holidays for whatever reason.

We believe that laughing—and even just smiling—can help get past even the most difficult of problems. That's why they say that laughter is the best medicine. It releases endorphins—known as "the pleasure chemical" —which are only released through laughter, eating chocolate and having sex.

We decided that of those three choices, providing you with laughter would be the safest and least dangerous for all of us. We just want to make fun of holiday stress and we certainly hope that you want to do the same.

In this book, we try to take a whimsical look at each holiday, even the religious holidays. Needless to say, we respect each and every religion and belief, but we feel it's also important to have a sense of humor. It's important to be able to laugh at ourselves, not in a mean way, but in an inclusive way that lets us see the humor in what we all do and how we all think.

If anything we say happens to challenge your sensibilities, or somehow offends you, please know that is not our intention. Every person has a different way of dealing with stress, and ours is to take a humorous approach. Our hearts go out to everyone who struggles during holiday time, and if our humor is challenging to you in any way, please don't take it personally. We sure don't!

Wishing you all Happy and Healthy Holidays!

With Much Love,
XOXOX
Jeffrey and Otakara

P.S. As our thanks for buying this book, we would love to give you a mini version of Jeffrey's hit book **Man Robs Bank With His Chin.**

Visit https://www.comedymatterstv.com/free/ for your FREE download!

NEW YEAR'S EVE

Theoretically, if we were going in order, we should technically start with New Year's Day, but we're going to claim poetic license even though this is not a poem, and start with what leads into New Year's Day … New Year's Eve.

New Year's Eve probably causes as much stress as any other holiday, if not more. And the stresses are probably equally the same for men and women.

First of all, after evaluating all you've accomplished or did NOT accomplish over the past year, and either categorizing yourself as a winner or loser, it makes you get the feeling that you have to have plans. Because what's New Year's Eve without plans, right? If you don't have plans on New Year's Eve it's like telling the world that you're a loser. Who doesn't have plans for New Year's Eve? (Read sarcastically!)

And if you're going to make plans you have to have someone to make them with, right? So now you have

7

to get some friends. And where are you going to get those elusive things that go by the name of friends? When you were just a kid you always had a group of friends. But as you got older and started to do things in life you tended to drift apart.

Now it's a month before New Year's Eve and you're in a panic. How do you make friends in a month? You either have to start making new friends or re-connect with your old ones. And that's where Facebook comes in.

Frantically you start looking up old friends from high school. The only ones you can find are all married with little kids, or else they aged very badly and really look old. And needless to say, you wouldn't want people to know that you're the same age.

Also, people tend to think it's a little weird to hear from someone they haven't spoken to in 15 years who suddenly asks what they're doing for New Year's. It can easily feel like most people have huge groups of friends except for you, and if the friend situation isn't bad enough, you also feel like you have to get a date.

Who are you going to kiss at midnight if you don't have a date? Whether you're a guy or a girl, you might wind up standing next to someone of the same sex, and that could be awkward, depending on your sexual proclivity.

So where do you get a date if you're not in a relationship at the moment and maybe haven't been in one since high school, or college?

Back to Facebook trying to track down the people you thought were cute back in high school or college. If you're lucky enough to find them on there, it usually turns out that they're not as cute as they used to be. Chances are you're not either.

If you're not dating anyone special, it can be tricky asking people out for that night. If you're a man and you're single, … and desperate, … do you take a chance and ask out that cute waitress from the diner you frequent, or the cute teller at the bank who always seems so friendly when you come in and asks you about your day even though you only came in to break a twenty?

If you're a woman and single and really don't want to stay home on New Year's Eve do you accept a date with that dweeb who's the only guy who had the nerve to ask you out?

First of all, on New Year's Eve everything is three times the usual cost, if not more. And night clubs and party rooms fill up quickly.

Then there's the outfit. Depending on where you're going you have to have a special New Year's Eve outfit. A regular everyday outfit just won't do, especially if you're trying to impress that special someone. And maybe not so much if you're a guy, because most guys these days dress like they're trying to appear homeless, but if you're a woman on New Year's Eve you want to be wearing something special. Preferably something new!

Then there's transportation. Do I drive or not drive? That is the question! If you live in a small town in Idaho maybe you could drive. Maybe it's even a tractor and can't go too fast. If you live in New York City you take your life in your hands just walking, so maybe you call an Uber or rent a limo, depending on two things: your finances, and how many people you'll be with.

How you decide to travel will also impact your decision on how much to drink or whether to drink at all. Your date, if you can find one, may expect champagne! Ka-ching!!!

And at the end of the night do you go home, or do you take a hotel room? If it's your first date you might want to re-think the hotel room thing because chances are you won't get your money back on New Year's Eve if your plans don't work out the way you wanted them to.

If you went out by yourself and got hammered in a local bar or a party you wound up getting invited to, do you believe the person you met who's just as hammered as you if not more so, who tells you they love you after only knowing you for two hours?

A WHIMSICAL HISTORY OF NEW YEAR S EVE

You'd have to go all the way back 4,000 years to ancient Babylon (which is quite a trip by the way) in order to find the earliest recorded celebration of a new year. The celebration was called Ikatu and was one of the oldest recorded Mesopotamian festivals.

In those days, the Babylonians celebrated the New Year not in January, but in late March, on the first new moon following the vernal equinox, which is not the name of a man, a gym or a disease.

It's the day when there's an equal amount of sunlight and darkness, and they had a huge religious festival which went on for 11 days, with a different ritual each day.

Besides celebrating the new year, it was also a celebration in honor of the Babylonian sky god Marduk, who supposedly defeated the evil sea goddess known as Tiamat.

Marduk was said to have created the world out of chaos! So that's who's to blame! I've been trying to figure that out for years! The festival was supposedly a way to prevent Marduk from taking back control of the world.

There was also an important political process tied in with these festivities as it was the time they would choose a new king or renew the current ruler's reign if they so wished.

Interestingly enough, it was also the tradition during this time to "humble" the king. This took place on the 4th day of the festival by (believe it or not) having the high priest first strip the king of his crown and other regalia.

At that point he would pull him by his ears to kneel down in front of a particular statue, (this is true!) and then have the king pray for forgiveness and promise that he had not been in dereliction of his duties.

As if that wasn't enough, when that was done, the head priest had to slap the king's face as hard as he could with an open hand, hopefully drawing tears from the king. (Google this if you don't believe us!)

If it, in fact, drew tears from the king it would prove than he was humble and that he was Marduk's choice to be king for another year.

This symbolic taking away of the king's power was supposed to strengthen the bond between the community and the gods, and prove to the king that without his crown, his sword and other regalia that he was just an ordinary mortal and that his fate depended upon the gods and how he served his people.

Supposedly, according to the Jerusalem Post, even a powerful Babylonian king like Nebuchadnezzar, which is a name you don't hear used much these days, and who considered himself king of kings, allowed himself to be slapped once a year.

And for his sin of destroying the First Temple of Jerusalem, The Temple of King Solomon, in 567 BC, Nebuchadnezzar, or Nebuch as his friends called him, is forever associated with the Jewish holiday of Purim, which commemorates the saving of the Jewish people by Queen Esther from a plot to destroy them by a vicious, bigoted man named Haman.

Throughout history many civilizations developed sophisticated calendars like Julius Caesar and his Julian calendar, in which he had to add 90 extra days to the year 46 B.C. in order to have the Roman calendar match with the movements of the sun.

Very often these civilizations would tie the first day of the year to some astronomical or agricultural event. For example, in ancient Egypt the year began with the annual flooding of the Nile River, which just happened to coincide with the rising of the star Sirius. I wonder if that's where Sirius XM radio got started?

14

In China however, they tied their first day of the New Year to the second new moon after the winter solstice and I tend to believe them, because Chinese people are the smartest people in the world. They have to be. They figured out how to speak Chinese! And even more impressive ... to write it!!! Chinese may be the Rubik's cube of languages!

There are still some countries that have Spring festivals and in Iran, March 21st is known as Nowruz, or New Year!

INTERESTING FACTS ABOUT NEW YEAR S EVE

1. Pope Gregory XIII introduced the Gregorian calendar in 1582 and named it after himself. In spite of that The Gregorian calendar is the most widely used calendar in the world. It often refers to this holiday as Old Year's Day, and in some places in the world it's called Saint Sylvester's Day.

2. In the United States, there are New Year's celebrations in every town, but the biggest and best is the so-called ball drop at the stroke of midnight in Times Square right in the middle of Manhattan. The ball itself weighs 11,875 pounds, which makes it hard for the average man to carry, and is covered in panels made of Waterford crystal. It's lowered down 70 feet on a pole reaching the roof of One Times Square in exactly 60 seconds.

3. Why we drop the ball is a story unto itself. Speaking as a proud resident of Manhattan, before 1904 New Year's Eve was always celebrated at Trinity Church on lower Broadway, in the Wall Street area which was established back in 1696.

The chiming of the church bells signaled the start of the New Year. But after 1904 the festivities were moved to the New York Times building further uptown. By the way, an even more interesting fact, none of the original parishioners still attend services there. It's all new people.

In those early days at the New York Times building they had no bells, so they used to use fireworks to signal the start of the new year. They realized they needed to change that when hot ashes fell down on the public below. Not a good thing! As a result, the police department then put a ban on using fireworks.

They needed a new approach, so the New York Times' chief electrician was asked to come up with something new to draw in the people. He was inspired by the old-time sailor's tradition of dropping what they called a "time ball" so sailors could adjust their chronometers while at sea.

Please don't ask me to explain that as I have no idea how that worked, and I'm not even sure what a chronometer is, but as of 1907, it led to the tradition of dropping a lit-up fancy ball on New Year's Eve.

4. Many people feel obliged to sing a song called Auld Lang Syne on New Year's Eve as a tradition, which is strange because it's a Scottish folk song made popular by the famous bandleader Guy Lombardo. He made it part of his annual New Year's Eve celebration starting in 1929. (For those of you who know it, you can vouch for the fact that it's not an easy song to dance to.)

Those were the days before television (believe it or not, there actually were such days), when everything was celebrated on the radio.

Guy Lombardo's band had developed a huge following. People didn't have a lot to do in those days and families would gather around the radio. You had to be very thin to get an entire family around one radio, but there wasn't as much food available in those days due to "The Great Depression", so I guess people were a lot smaller then.

Guy Lombardo was originally from western Ontario in Canada where there was a large Scottish population, and it was traditional for bands to end their sets by playing Auld Lang Syne. In Life magazine back in 1965 he was quoted as saying, "When we left Canada we had no idea we would ever play it again." He too understood that people thought it was "corny".

The tradition continues to this very day. For many people, New Year's Eve wouldn't be the same without it.

5. The Times Square celebration started in 1907 and usually has at least 1,000,000 people attending which makes it crazy for the NYPD. People start gathering hours before the event and once they're in they can't

really leave, no matter how cold it gets and even if they have to pee. Some people actually wear diapers to prevent disaster. As a native New Yorker, I attended once in person and found it very claustrophobic so I generally just watch it on TV.

6. It was the first broadcast on the radio in 1928 and again thanks to Guy Lombardo was on CBS TV for 20 years, from 1956-1976.

7. After Guy Lombardo passed away in 1977, Dick Clark took over the festivities with New Year's Rockin' Eve which he had started on NBC in 1973, and which he did for the next 33 years on ABC until he retired in 2006 due to illness. At that time Ryan Seacrest took over the reins of the show. Dick Clark did guest appearances until his passing in 2012.

8. New Year's Eve is celebrated differently all over the world. It's a public holiday in places like the Philippines, and Latvia and in Japan, it's considered a government holiday.

NEW YEAR'S DAY (AKA WHAT HAPPENED LAST NIGHT DAY)

This day often sets the tone for the entire year. First, we have to wake up and that's not always easy. Especially if we live alone. If you live with another human, they can assist in bringing you back to life. For some of us it's not actually waking up, it's coming to!

Sometimes we wake up next to someone who doesn't look familiar to us and that is a special experience ... especially if you're married. That conversation can be kind of awkward.

If you're single it's less of a problem. But you still have to re-introduce yourself, and ask the other person their name, assuming you actually did introduce yourself in the first place the night before. #extremelyawkward

Then we have to find a nice way to ask that person to leave, but not before checking our valuables to make sure that everything is still there.

And then once we're alone, we must attempt to remember where we were and what we did, by piecing together parts of the previous evening, sometimes using credit card receipts to help us recall where we were the night before, and who, if anyone, we might have to apologize to.

Sometimes it helps when a friend calls to say those magic words, "you wouldn't believe what you did last night", and that's one particularly painful way of finding out the truth.

New Year's Day is also the day when after we regain our senses, or what's left of them, we resolve to make certain positive changes in our lives, or what we call "New Year's Resolutions." We all make them, really good ones too like:

1. I will work harder this year, despite the fact that working gives me hives.

2. I will finally lose those last 20 pounds I've been trying to lose since 1954.

3. I will join a gym.

4. I will take French lessons (can also be Spanish,

Chinese, or Japanese lessons).

5. I will go to sleep earlier and wake up earlier.

6. I will be more careful with who I date and try to have more respect for myself.

7. For the men - no more strip clubs - I must stop being so gullible and realize that those girls don't really like me. They just act like they do.

8. I won't be so argumentative … and don't you dare tell me I can't do this!

9. I will be grateful for what I have and not be so envious of other people.

10. I will try to be a better person in every way.

And we all break them, in differing amounts of time. Some of us break them the day we make them. Others of us make valiant attempts to live up to them, like buying a gym membership to get that dream body we always wanted, and some of us even show up there once or twice, hoping to achieve that body in one major workout session.

A WHIMSICAL HISTORY OF NEW YEAR S DAY

Back in the day when Mesopotamia was still considered a cool place to hang out, which was probably around 2000 B.C., they celebrated the start of the new year in mid-March.

It was celebrated with an all-out 11-day festival, and when I say "all out" I mean it. There are some people who still have not recovered from it, and that's a long time to have a hangover.

As explained on History.com, the people celebrated the sky god Marduk's religious victory over the sea goddess Tiamat, who, according to local legend, was not the easiest woman to get along with, so it was considered quite an accomplishment to best her.

Julius Caesar who was basically in charge at the time was convinced by a man named Sosigenes who happened to be an astrologer, that they should follow the solar year instead of the lunar cycle, which is very different than a unicycle.

Starting with 46 B.C. the new year was officially started in January. The length of the year also increased from about ten months to 365 1/4 days. Caesar wound up adding 67 days to 45 B.C. making

46 B.C. start as of January 1, the very first New Year's Day of all time.

January was named after the god Janus, who was said to have had two faces. If that was so, he would have done very well in politics today. But since he was said to have had two faces, he was able to look into the past and the future at the same time, which would give most normal people a headache. I guess that's why he was a god. It didn't seem to bother him at all.

INTERESTING FACTS ABOUT NEW YEAR S DAY

1. The celebration of this day goes back to ancient Rome under the Julian calendar named for and proposed by Julius Caesar in 45 BC. The day was originally dedicated to the god Janus - the god of beginnings - for whom January is named after.

2. It's probably the most celebrated holiday in the world.

3. Julius Caesar was the one who decreed that every four years a day be added to February, the shortest month to keep his calendar in synch.

4. Before his assassination in 44 B.C., which had nothing to do with him changing the calendar and causing all that confusion, he also changed the name of the month Quintilis to Julius, which became July after himself.

5. His successor Augustus took the next month which had been named Sextilis and changed that to August. I wonder which emperor was named May or April.

6. It wasn't until the 1570's that Pope Gregory XIII tried to fix the calendar problems by asking yet another astronomer Christopher Clavius to come

up with a new calendar which he did and which is known as the Gregorian calendar. It seems like in those days people were very fond of naming things after themselves! He again seconded Julius Caesar's idea that leap year only happens once every four years. Apologies to those born on February 29th!

7. During the Middle Ages the celebration of New Year's Day fell out of favor, and those who did celebrate did not always do so on January 1. They must have been geniuses in those days because they figured out that Caesar and Sosigenes messed up their calculations. They said the solar year was 365.242199 days and not 365.25 days which led to an 11 minute a year difference. That one error alone added seven days by the year 1,000, and ten days by the mid-15th century. And this was all done without computers! How?

8. In 1582, they finally implemented the Gregorian calendar omitting ten days for that year, and officially adding one day every four years on Feb. 29th for leap year. Since that time January 1 has been the official celebration of New Year's Day.

VALENTINE'S DAY

Around the end of January those of us who are single start to get nervous about the impending date of February 14th that is coming up all too quickly: Valentine's Day, otherwise known as the scourge of the single human being!

This was a holiday that must have been invented by florists and candy makers, because they both make a fortune out of other people's misery.

Single men in particular start wondering how they can find a Valentine in a couple of weeks when they haven't had a girlfriend in years. And single women start planning on where they can hide that day so that they don't have to admit to their friends and co-workers that they don't have a Valentine.

Some women go so far as to send themselves flowers with no name attached so that it looks like it came from an anonymous secret admirer.

This works especially well if you have a doorman building so that when you walk into the lobby your doorman presents them to you with a card from "your anonymous admirer!"

And if you're not single and do have that "significant other", which is the politically correct way of naming who you exchange body fluids with, you have to start planning what you are going to do for that person to make them know that they didn't make a mistake, and that you are the right choice for them.

If you are in a relationship, and it hasn't been going particularly well, brace yourself for what might be a break-up just before Valentine's Day.

Some people don't want to buy expensive gifts for someone they're not getting along with, but still haven't had the nerve to engage in "the breakup conversation."

The pressure builds up intensely until just before the holiday when they are forced to choose between spending big bucks or being honest!

At the last minute many people will opt to save the money!

In the event the breakup goes down, Valentine's Day will be a particularly cruel and punishing day for you, surrounded by hearts, love messages and don't forget that every song on the radio will remind you of that certain person you're trying not to think about.

In most relationships one person usually feels stronger than the other when it comes to feelings. A woman may just be tolerating the guy, so as not to be alone, but he's planning on proposing to her on Valentine's Day. He may have even bought a ring. That's a tough one. How do you turn down someone with a marriage proposal without entirely destroying their self-esteem?

I think it's always safest to blame yourself. "It's not you, it's ME!" Tell them you have a fear of commitment, that you don't deserve them, and that they're too good for you. Finding the right excuse is difficult, but if you think hard you'll be able to come up with one, even if it's something simple like your significant other thinking its pronounced "Valentimes Day." That would be a deal-breaker for me and for a lot of other people I'm sure!

A WHIMSICAL HISTORY OF VALENTINE S DAY

No one is exactly sure why, but for some reason, the month of February has long been associated with romance. St. Valentine's Day as we know it contains tradition taken from both Roman and Christian values.

As mentioned earlier, there were three different saints named Valentine according to the Catholic Church and if anyone would know it would be them! All three were martyred, which is a polite way of saying "killed."

The most interesting possibility for who inspired the romanticism of Valentine's Day was the Valentine who served as a priest under Emperor Claudius II in Rome during the third century, which was quite a while ago. When Claudius came to the conclusion that single men made better soldiers than ones who were married with children he decreed that no young men could get married any longer.

Valentine felt this wasn't fair and continued performing marriages, which were probably not as glamorous as they are today. They didn't even have electricity yet, and there were no limos for the wedding party. But anyway, Emperor Claudius caught an attitude when finding out that Valentine was still performing weddings and ordered that he be killed. Which he was, because in those days people did what Claudius ordered them to do.

Another version of how Valentine's Day came into being was that Valentine may have been "martyred" for trying to help Christians escape from Roman prisons. They were not treating them as well as one might expect for a prison in ancient times. Most prisons in those days had a rack and other instruments of torture, which made imprisonment really something to not look forward to.

(And by the way if any of you know why they refer to them as "instruments" please feel free to contact us with the information. To my knowledge no one plays the rack, or the Iron Maiden. However, there was a rock group in the 60's named Iron Maiden!)

There's yet another version that has Valentine in prison himself, and sending what would turn out to be the very first Valentine's Day card to a girl he fell in love with, which is not easy to do in an ancient prison. How did you even meet a girl in those days? Even if you saw someone you were attracted to, it wasn't like you could ask them for their number. In those days when people said, "I hope to see you again", they really meant it!

33

Some say this girl may have been the daughter of his jailer, who visited Valentine during his confinement, up until the time he was killed. After he was killed she abruptly stopped visiting. But supposedly his letter or card to her was signed "From Your Valentine."

No matter which of these accounts may be true, the common thread is that whoever Valentine was, he was a romantic at heart! By the time the Middle Ages rolled around, which was really a time of fun and games … if you liked plagues, filth and torture, Valentine was one of the most popular saints in Western Europe.

There's a whole other theory that Valentine's Day was an effort to "Christianize" a pagan holiday that fell at the "Ides of February" which was February 15th. It was known as Lupercalia and it was a fertility festival dedicated to the Roman god of agriculture, a guy named Faunus. No last name, just Faunus!

It was also held in honor of the supposed founders of Rome, Romulus and Remus, twin brothers in Roman mythology, each of whom wanted to build their own city. Romulus reportedly killed Remus and founded Rome on April 1, 753, which was probably before most of you were even born. For Remus, it was the absolute worst April Fools prank of all time!

To tie in the romantic angle, during the festival a priest would sacrifice a goat for fertility and a dog for purification. Where was PETA when you needed them?

Then they would cut the goat's hide into strips dipped in the goat's blood and go through the streets slapping women and crop fields with the strips (how do you slap a crop field?) and the women loved it because it was supposed to make them more fertile.

Later in the day all the women in the city would put their names in a big pot and the city's bachelors would pick a name, like they were playing the lottery, and they would spend the next year together as a couple. Many of them wound up getting married, hence the connection to romance.

Fortunately, these days you can just buy your best girl a card and some candy and no goats, dogs, or blood-soaked strips of hide have to be involved. Unless your girl insists!

As it turns out, Lupercalia was outlawed at the end of the 5th century by Pope Gelasius who declared it "un-Christian" and made February 14th Valentine's Day.

During the Middle Ages the people of France and England believed that February 14th was the beginning of birds' mating season, which further connected the day to the idea of romance.

The first appearance of written Valentines greetings occurred in 1415, and it was a poem of all things written by a man named Charles, the Duke of Orleans. He wrote it to his wife while he was imprisoned in the Tower of London after being captured at the Battle of Agincourt, which I know you're all familiar with. Why it was considered a Valentine, as opposed to just a love poem no one knows, but maybe he mailed it on February 14th.

Actually, it's not even certain they had mail in those days. Maybe he sent it by carrier pigeon. Rumor has it that years later King Henry V went out and hired a writer to send a Valentine to a woman who went by the name of Catherine of Valois, but you knew that already.

These days if you send someone a poem, it better be amazing, or you're liable to be institutionalized!

Valentine's Day is also celebrated in Mexico, France, England, Canada, and Australia. In England it got really big in the 1600's, around the time that chivalry was taking off. By the 1700's everybody was exchanging handwritten notes and small gifts. But by 1900 they began to exchange printed cards, which made it easier for shy people to express their feelings for someone of the opposite sex. Same sex cards weren't really a thing yet.

It wasn't until the 1840's that an enterprising woman named Esther Howland, who is known as "The Mother of the Valentine" began making and selling mass produced cards that were elaborately decorated with lace, pictures, and colorful ribbons.

Thanks to Esther these days more than one billion Valentine's Day cards are sent each year, with 85% of them purchased by women.

INTERESTING FACTS ABOUT VALENTINE S DAY

1. It's also known as Saint Valentine's Day or The Feast of Saint Valentine. It's a celebration of love and affection, and is observed by people in many countries, not just the United States.

2. For some reason many Christian martyrs were named Valentine. It's a dangerous name, so keep that in mind unless you're planning to become a Christian martyr.

   One of the Valentines was Valentine of Rome, a priest who was martyred in 269 and was added to the calendar of Saints by Pope Galesius in 496 and buried on Feb. 14th in a place called Via Flaminia.

3. The other Valentine was Valentine of Terni. He was martyred in the super exciting year of 273 thanks to Emperor Aurelian who it seems had an aversion to Christians. He too was buried on the Via Flaminia. Coincidence? I think not!!!

4. Some even say there was a third Valentine, who may or may not have been martyred in Africa along with some other unfortunate people, but nothing more is known about him, except that he died. Coincidentally all the people who lived in that era have died.

5. Rumor has it that Saint Valentine was interrogated by none other than Roman Emperor Claudius II himself, in order to try and convince him to give up Christianity and convert to Roman Paganism. Saint Valentine tried to convince the Emperor to convert to Christianity which didn't sit well with the Emperor, who then felt compelled to kill him. Which he did!

6. Before his execution, as a show of the power of Jesus, Saint Valentine supposedly healed the blind daughter of his jailer and restored her sight which caused her 46-member family to get baptized and follow Jesus. Unfortunately, he was still executed anyway. The Emperor was a hard man to impress. Not even curing blindness did it for him! And that's not easy to do! Some people don't know how to show their gratitude.

7. It's only recently that Valentine's Day has become associated with love. The Day of Love was traditionally celebrated on March 12, known as Saint Gregory's Day, or Feb. 22nd otherwise known as Saint Vincent's Day.

8. Historians claim that the first recorded association of V-Day with romance is in a poem by Geoffrey Chaucer in 1382. He's the guy who wrote "The Wife of Bath", which was part of The Canterbury Tales, written in Old English.

9. They also say that the earliest description of Feb. 14th as an annual celebration of love appears in something called "The Charter of the Court of Love" supposedly issued by Charles VI of France which described lavish festivities including jousting, song and poetry competition, and wild dancing. Just like today, when jousting is making a comeback. All over the country men are asking each other, "Would you care to joust?"

10. It's estimated that approximately 190 million Valentine's Day cards are sent each year in the USA alone. And they're all to the same woman! (Just kidding. It's really two women!) They say that half of them are sent to family members other than husband and wife, most often they are to children. Teachers receive most of the Valentines that children make in school.

11. The average amount of money spent on V-Day in America is approximately $131 per person as of 2013. I'm guessing that most of these people probably don't live in New York! In New York you can have a nice lunch for that amount of money!

EASTER

WHICH OF THESE DOES NOT BELONG?

Easter is a very special Christian holiday commemorating the resurrection of Jesus Christ who according to the New Testament rose from the dead three days after he was crucified by the Romans in 30 A.D. He was only 33 years old.

And that was only one of his miracles. He had turned

water into wine which made him very popular at parties, and he had even walked on water without ruining his sandals. He healed the sick and fed a multitude of 5,000 people with only five loaves of bread and two fish. They don't say what size portion each person got, but nevertheless, it was still a true miracle.

The holiday itself begins with Lent, a 40-day period of fasting, prayer and sacrifice during which people who celebrate the holiday must give up something they enjoy.

Many kids in my neighborhood used to make believe they enjoyed things they didn't like so they didn't have to give up something they really did like. One of my friends tried giving up prunes and Lima beans for Lent, but his parents didn't go for it.

The holiday ends with Holy Week which includes Holy Thursday, the celebration of Jesus' Last Supper with his 12 disciples, Good Friday which observes Jesus' death, and Easter Sunday.

As it's written in the New Testament Jesus was arrested by Roman authorities because he claimed to be the "Son of God." Other historians say they just felt his popularity was becoming a threat to the Empire, and not the one starring Terence Howard and Taraji P. Henson.

It was Pontius Pilate the prefect, whatever that is, in the province of Judea who will forever be guilty of sentencing Jesus to death by crucifixion, one of the cruelest methods of punishment in those days. It took place at Calvary in 30 A.D.

On a personal note, as a child growing up in the Bronx, in New York City, it was literally a frightening sight for me to see people wearing crucifixes around their necks. Not being familiar with that religion as a young child, I thought it was a warning of some kind. Once it was explained to me the truth of what it was, it was even more upsetting that anyone could do that to a person.

It was actually a representation of the way in which Jesus died. He was crucified and people all over the world are wearing a reenactment of the way in which he was killed. Millions and millions of people around the world wear that symbol. Had he been killed in any other way, people might not have been able to wear it.

It was his resurrection three days later that convinced people and especially his followers that he was the "Son of God." No one else has been able to do that either before or since.

And because Jesus' arrest occurred during the Jewish holiday of Passover, both holidays usually occur close to each other in the Judeo-Christian calendar.

The name of the holiday was actually taken from the name of an ancient pagan goddess, Eastre who was the goddess of spring. In those days women had all the power, and it was generally acknowledged by the fact of people worshipping the different goddesses. Eastre's pagan symbol was the rabbit. These days ... for those of you who know ... it can have a completely different meaning!

To make it easier for the early Christians to convert the early Teutonic (German) tribes to Christianity, they adopted their festival of Eastre, and just changed the meaning and purpose of the celebration. I guess the Teutonic tribesmen were easily fooled in those days. Maybe they just weren't paying attention.

It definitely helped that the festival of Eastre was very close to the day of Jesus' resurrection anyway, so that probably made it a little bit easier to convince them. The early Teutonic tribes often gave each other eggs as a symbol of birth and renewal hence the tradition of Easter eggs.

And Eastre's symbol of the hare or rabbit was supposedly an egg-laying animal, hence the origin of the Easter Bunny!

In 325 A.D. Emperor Constantine met with church leaders and decreed that Easter would fall on the first Sunday after the first full moon after the Spring or Vernal Equinox.

But to this day it gets celebrated at different times in different places around the world.

EASTER IN THE CZECH REPUBLIC

Easter is celebrated differently all over the world. In many places, the tradition is combined with the pagan tradition of celebrating Spring.

I, Otakara, was born and raised in the Czech Republic where Easter has a very different tone. So different in fact that it often raises the eyebrows of American feminists. Why you might ask? Because girls and women are whipped with long whips made of elaborately braided pussy willows!

And believe it or not, the women actually want that. Not only do they want it, they demand it! It's part of what they do to celebrate the holiday.

The whole celebration of Easter starts by giving funny names to the days prior to Easter Monday which is the final and the most important day in the Czech Republic.

Ugly Wednesday is named after Judas, who must have been very ugly to have a day named after his appearance, or maybe it refers to his act of betraying Jesus. That was pretty ugly too!

Green Thursday doesn't have to do anything with being eco-friendly, but people do help the environment by fasting or eating only green veggies to honor the Last Supper. What green veggies have to do with The Last Supper I have absolutely no idea, but I have a feeling it's tied in with the day being called Green Thursday.

Why Good Friday is called "good" is also a mystery to me, because Jesus had a particularly hard time that day, but just so you know the direct translation from Czech is Big Friday which, I think, makes a little bit more sense. Big Bad Friday might make even more sense!

White Saturday was named to symbolize light in general, and Jesus' resurrection. Light always symbolizes knowledge and all positive things. We strive to bring light into our lives.

On White Saturday boys and men in the villages walk from house to house equipped with unusual instrument-like things that make an annoying rattling sound. So annoying in fact that they hope the inhabitants of the house will give them money just to stop!

They say they do this to scare off Judas, but if that's the case, their timing is off by about 2,000 years. Truthfully, the real purpose is to get money from the people to leave them alone. This is the Czech version of "Trick or Treat".

In America, you give people the choice of Trick or Treat. In the Czech Republic they start off with the "trick" and stay there until they wear you down and you give them the "treat!"

Easter Sunday is spent with the girls coloring eggs and the boys and men making those pussy willow whips. Those whips are no joke either. The bigger the better, made out of anywhere from between 4 to 16 branches braided together to get the maximum sting.

Interestingly enough the men would judge each other on the width and length of their whips! (Sound familiar?) This answers the age-old question, "Does size matter?" In the Czech Republic the answer is definitely "Yes!"

All this is leading up to Easter Monday which to Czechs is the real holiday. From early morning to the evening, boys walk from door to door and whip girls and women in their homes. The women don't have to leave their homes. The whipping service comes to them. That's what you call door-to-door service.

In exchange for the whipping, the boys and men used to receive colored eggs, or in more modern times some chocolates for their excellent whipping service. Girls appreciate this because they are taught that the whipping is supposed to keep them healthy and fertile. This definitely would not go over big in America today.

In the afternoon the grown up men … those with the biggest whips … head out and receive a colorful ribbon on the top of their whip (the more houses visited, the more ribbons they get!), plus they get a shot of hard liquor. Very often it's strong plum brandy.

By late in the afternoon between the whipping and the brandy some men don't even know where they are anymore. I grew up in Moravia where this whole thing is taken very seriously, so I've experienced it firsthand.

At some point, the wives of the men who did the whipping have to go out and search for their husbands, often finding them lying on the side of the road in a ditch, or passed out in someone else's home, depending on how much plum brandy they actually imbibed.

Then they have to figure out how to get them home.

Slovakia takes the whipping one step further. As if being whipped was not enough, they also douse girls with a bucket of water, and again this is all with the girl's consent. In the USA if you dare to wet a girl's hair or her outfit, trust me, she will be whipping YOU!

1. Easter falls on a different date each year, because Easter, Ash Wednesday, and Palm Sunday are considered "moveable feasts."

2. In Western Christianity which goes by the Gregorian calendar, the holiday always falls on a Sunday somewhere between March 22nd and April 25th.

3. In Eastern Christianity which uses the Julian calendar, the holiday falls on a Sunday between April 4th and May 8th.

4. Although inherently a Christian holiday, many of Easter's traditions are tied to pagan celebrations and, believe it or not, to the Jewish holiday of Passover.

5. The Last Supper, which occurred the night before Jesus was arrested by the Romans, who felt that he was a threat to the empire, was actually a Passover feast.

6. It was at that feast that Jesus identified the Matzoh, or unleavened bread, he was sharing with his disciples as his "body" and the wine they drank as his "blood."

7. These symbolic elements became the basis for the Christian ritual of Holy Communion, which is a part of every Christian church service.

8. Palm Sunday commemorates Jesus' arrival in Jerusalem and it's called Palm Sunday because his followers laid palm leaves across the road to greet him.

9. The tradition of coloring eggs for Easter (Easter Eggs) was based in pagan traditions pre-dating Christianity when the egg represented fertility and birth and possibly relates to rebirth or resurrection.

10. Candy and chocolate eggs are often delivered to children by an "Easter Bunny". Some historians believe that particular tradition is tied to German immigrants who came over in the 1700's and looked at rabbits as being associated with procreation and birth. Roman Catholicism became the dominant religion in Germany during the 15th century.

11. Easter in Greek is called "Pascha" which is the Greek transliteration of the Aramaic form of the Hebrew word "Pesach" which means Passover.

12. The word "Pesach" comes from a word that means leap, dance, or hop, referring to the Angel

of Death passing or jumping over Jewish homes, which is celebrated during the holiday of Passover.

13. Pascha starts with Easter Sunday and ends 40 days later with a holiday known as the "Feast of the Ascension." But the Jewish people had the tradition of sacrificing what they called a "Paschal lamb" the night before Passover. Coincidence? I think not!

14. Lamb also holds significance for both religions. Jesus is sometimes referred to as the "lamb of God," referring to his being sacrificed, and lamb is often served at both Easter and Passover dinners.

PASSOVER

✡ ✡ ✡ ✡

Passover is a Jewish holiday commemorating the liberation of the Jewish people from slavery in ancient Egypt, and their freedom as a nation under the leadership and guidance of Moses who led them wandering through the desert over a period of 40 years.

They had no GPS or Waze in those days and Moses may have had a bad sense of direction to have been wandering for forty years. Most deserts in those days did not have any comfort stations, and many people have said that if only Moses had just gone in the other direction the Jewish people could have wound up with all the oil!

Passover is a week-long holiday with the first two nights being celebrated with a big meal called a "Seder" during which the story of Passover is read from a book called the "Hagaddah". At the seder several traditions take place.

The youngest child asks what are known as "the four questions" which are there in order to create curiosity in the children at the table and make them feel part of the holiday. The main question is, "Why is this night different from all other nights?"

This is followed by four other questions read either in Hebrew or in English:

    a. "Why is it that on all other nights during the year we eat either bread or matzoh, but on this night we eat only matzoh?" The answer is after the Pharaoh finally agreed to let the Jews go after enduring ten plagues set upon the Egyptian people by God, the Jews were in such a hurry to leave that they had no time to let their dough rise and bake their bread. They took the raw dough with them on the desert and had to settle for unleavened bread, or crackers which they called "Matzoh." Eating matzoh on the holiday reminds them of their struggle.

b. "Why is it that on all other nights we eat all kinds of herbs, but on this night we eat only bitter herbs?" The answer is that the bitter herbs, known as "Maror," are a reminder of the bitterness of slavery and how the Jewish people suffered under the Pharaoh of Egypt.

c. "Why is it that on all other nights we do not dip our herbs even once, but on this night, we dip them twice?" The answer is that parsley represents new life and salt water represents the tears of Hebrew slaves and how hard they worked in ancient Egypt. They also dip the herbs in something called "Charoset" which is a mixture of chopped apples, nuts, and honey which reminds them of the clay used to make bricks for the Pharaoh's buildings. And if you've ever eaten any of this stuff, it's delicious, but it lays in your stomach like one of Pharaoh's buildings!

d. "Why is it that on all other nights we eat either sitting or reclining, but on this night, we eat in a reclining position?" The answer is that leaning on a pillow signifies the comforts of freedom and the ability to choose how we want to live, thanks to the hardship our ancestors had to endure.

The first two questions remind the people of the burdens of slavery. The second two questions both symbolize and remind the people of the glory of freedom.

A WHIMSICAL HISTORY OF PASSOVER

Once upon a time, there were 12 tribes of Israel. There was a man named Joseph, a founder of one of those tribes, who was the son of Jacob and Rachel, and one of the 12 brothers who lived in the land of Canaan. He was his father's preferred son, and hence the receiver of his "coat of many colors."

Because of jealousy his brothers hated him and sold him into slavery in Egypt telling their father he had been killed! Nice guys! No brothers have been that close since Cain and Abel.

While imprisoned in Egypt, Joseph was recognized for his ability to interpret dreams, and he interpreted a dream for the Pharaoh that saved the Pharaoh from a great famine.

For that Joseph was freed and elevated to a position of Vizier, the second most powerful man in Egypt except for the Pharaoh. Because Joseph was so powerful, he moved his family and tribe into Egypt. For many years they lived in harmony with the Egyptians, but eventually the Egyptians began to see them as a threat.

After Joseph died, the Pharaoh ordered the

imprisonment of the Jews and the drowning of their first-born sons in the Nile River. One of those doomed babies was put into a reed basket and set afloat on the water by his mother hoping to save his life.

As luck would have it the baby was rescued by the Pharaoh's daughter and adopted into the Egyptian royal family. That baby was Moses.

When Moses grew up, aside from having a fear of water, he became aware of his true identity as a Jew and how brutally the other Hebrews were being treated. He killed an Egyptian slave master and fled to the Sinai Peninsula where he lived for 40 years.

One day he got a message straight from God himself, not as a text message but in the form of a burning bush, making him the only man ever to see God, besides drunks. God told him to return to Egypt and ask Pharaoh to free his people.

Pharaoh, who goes unnamed in the Bible, refused multiple requests to let the Jewish people leave for just three days to celebrate a feast.

In anger and to teach Pharaoh a lesson, God unleashed ten plagues on the Egyptians. It included the waters of the rivers turning, to blood killing all the fish, a plague of frogs, followed by biting insects and wild animals, then livestock disease and boils, fiery hail, locusts, total darkness, and finally the one that made the Pharaoh give in, the death of the first born.

The Jews were instructed by God to mark their doors with the blood of a sacrificial lamb so the Angel of Death would "pass over" them, hence the name Passover. Thank God the Angel of Death didn't come from below or the holiday would have been called "Passunder" which doesn't sound nearly as good.

To this day this is why all Jewish homes mark their doors with a Mezuzah, that interesting little thing with biblical scrolls inside of it that you're supposed to kiss every time you pass through the doorway.

After that 10th plague the Pharaoh was convinced to let the Jewish people go, but right after he did he changed his mind and his troops chased them to bring them back.

The troops chased them to the edges of the Red Sea at which point God parted the seas to let the Jewish people escape and when the Egyptian troops tried to follow God closed the sea on top of them drowning all the troops.

Wow! What a story. It should be a movie! ... And it was. ... Charlton Heston played Moses in the 1956 movie "The Ten Commandments".

And so the Jewish people spent 40 years wandering

the desert, free, but very hot, until they reached the land of Canaan later on known as Israel, "The Promised Land." And that's when they invented air conditioning!

INTERESTING FACTS ABOUT PASSOVER

1. The number 40 recurs throughout the Bible as in 40 days and nights in Noah's great flood and the 40 days and nights that Moses spent on Mount Sinai, or the 40 years he had lived in Egypt. The number 40 recurs 146 times in the Bible.

2. The purpose of The Hagaddah or the book that Jewish people read from on this holiday is to encourage future generations of Jewish people to inquire about their history, especially the children.

3. One of the ten plagues unleashed by God on the Egyptian people to encourage Pharaoh to let the Jewish people go was total darkness. But there was no electricity in those days anyway, so how did he manage that? Every time someone lit a candle an angel blew it out?

4. Not only do you have to eat unleavened bread (Matzoh) during the holiday, but you must remove all leavened products of any kind from your home.

5. Gefilte fish is one of the things traditionally eaten at the seder, but no one has ever caught a Gefilte fish and no one really knows where they came

from. They do know that the horseradish used to spice up the Gefilte fish represents the sadness and bitterness of the slavery of the Jewish people in Egypt.

MOTHER'S DAY

Mother's Day is always celebrated on the second Sunday in May. It's celebrated in more than 40 countries, or wherever people have or have had mothers, and has been going on in the USA since the early 20th century.

I guess that before that no one cared too much about their mothers! So who was the genius who came up with the idea to honor all mothers and the concept of motherhood in general?

A man named Abe Bembelman somewhere in Europe in the 1500's was said to be very attached to his mother. He was also responsible for the invention of humming. Before Abe Bembelman people would hear a song, they liked and have absolutely no idea how to recall the tune. Then Abe invented humming, and it changed the world.

Buying a present for your Mom to show her that you're grateful that she had sex with your Dad, and let him get her pregnant, is a tricky thing. Cause what if you hate your Mom or if she hates you! That can happen.

Some people have to work hard to be grateful to their Mom because maybe she wasn't the best Mom while they were growing up. Moses' Mom put him in a basket and set him afloat in a river. Now that had to be a tough way to start out, but luckily, he turned that around, and it wound up turning out pretty good for him. Just check the Bible if you don't believe me!

In Roman mythology, Romulus and Remus' mom did the same thing and put both of her twins in a basket and sent it down the river. They were supposedly saved by a wolf who suckled them and made sure they survived.

Romulus went on to found the city of Rome. He didn't do too badly considering his original circumstances. Yet if he was around today he probably couldn't even get a seat in any of Rome's exclusive restaurants, unless he updated his wardrobe. Most restaurants don't have a cloak/spear checkroom!

So if anything good at all ever happened to you in your life, it was because your Mom got pregnant and you came into being, and that's how you have to look at it.

No one chooses their parents, although from the Spiritual point of view it's said we choose our parents from our "soul group" before we are born to learn lessons we didn't learn in a previous life.

Some of us must have been pretty bad in a previous life 'cause we had a lot of lessons to learn in this one.

Being a mother has to be a great thing because women all over the world have been doing that since the time of the Garden of Eden. Eve liked being a Mom so much that she supposedly had 63 children, according to some reports, 32 daughters and 31 sons. I guess that she and Adam didn't have that much else to do. And according to the Bible, there was a shortage of babysitters in the Garden of Eden, which made things even more difficult.

There were also no cell phones in those days, and no internet, so all they had to do was hang out with each other and make babies. I guess they felt the need to try and populate the earth.

That had to be rough for Eve on Mother's Day. Where would you even put all those presents? There was no Target or Walmart or really anything at all, so many people made their own gifts, usually out of bark.

Anyway, the stores are filled with all kinds of stuff for you to get your Mom. Remember you only get one Mom, and it's important to try and appreciate her, because one day she won't be there anymore, and it'll be too late to tell her all the things you wanted to tell her but never did.

The point of all this is to say, try and be grateful that you had a mother, and honor her on Mother's Day because if it weren't for her, you wouldn't even be reading this, and then what would you do?

A WHIMSICAL HISTORY OF MOTHER S DAY

Celebrations of mothers and motherhood, in general, go back to ancient times, as far back as the ancient Romans and Greeks. They actually held festivals in honor of two goddesses known as "the mother goddesses" named Rhea and Cybele.

In more modern times there was an early Christian festival known as Mothering Day which was held the fourth Sunday in Lent, and commemorated the return of the faithful at that time of year to their "mother church", referring to the main church nearest their home for a special service.

Mothering Day was popular mostly in the UK and certain parts of Europe. That holiday eventually morphed into a holiday where children would give their mothers presents, flowers and other gifts showing their appreciation for all their mother had done for them.

In 1868, after the Civil War Anna Jarvis' Mother's Day Work Club also attempted to bring about reconciliation between the North and the South through the mothers of soldiers on both sides. That's when she organized "Mother's Friendship Day."

There was another woman also influential in the development of the holiday, and her name was Julia Ward Howe who was both an abolitionist fighting slavery and a suffragette trying to get women the right to vote.

She wrote what became known as "The Mother's Day Proclamation" which encouraged mothers to promote world peace, and a few years later campaigned for a "Mother's Peace Day" that would fall every year on June 2. There was also a man who became known as "the father of Mother's Day" whose name was Frank Hering and he worked in conjunction with a woman named Mary Towles Sasseen to organize a Mother's Day during the late 19th and early 20th century.

Anna Jarvis got the financial backing for her first Mother's Day celebration, held in a Methodist church in Grafton West Virginia in 1908, from a department store owner in Philadelphia named John Wanamaker. Strictly by coincidence (or was it?) his stores were named Wanamakers!

In an unusual twist, Jarvis herself never married or had children. However, she was able to start a huge letter writing campaign to get the holiday made official by the government, which came to fruition in 1914 when President Woodrow Wilson made it official, to be held on the second Sunday in May.

Anna Jarvis' original idea was to celebrate the day by wearing a white carnation and visiting one's mother or attending a religious service. Not particularly a wild celebration.

But once it became a national holiday and florists, card companies, and candy companies got involved it turned into her worst nightmare, and she tried her best to get them to tone it down by denouncing what it had become, and trying to urge people not to participate.

By the time of her death in 1948 she had initiated several lawsuits against companies and groups that had used the name Mother's Day, and actually tried to get it removed from the American calendar. The holiday she created had wound up ruining her life.

INTERESTING FACTS ABOUT MOTHER S DAY

1. Mother's Day in this country was started in 1908 thanks to a woman named Anna Jarvis who wanted to honor her own Mom, Ann Reeves Jarvis who died in 1905, probably before many of you who are reading this book were even born!

2. Ann Reeves Jarvis was a nurse who was a peace activist (even in those days they had them … but I bet she didn't smoke weed!) who treated wounded soldiers on both sides of The Civil War.

3. She also created what were called "Mother's Day Work Clubs" to address public health issues and teach mothers how to properly care for their children. Hygiene was not much of a thing in those days.

4. Anna Jarvis rightly felt that "a mother is the person who has done more for you than anyone else in the world."

5. In 1912 Anna Jarvis trademarked the term "Mother's Day" and specified that it should be a singular possessive, so that each family honors it's own mother and not a plural possessive which would allow people to honor all mothers in the world at the same time.

6. Interestingly enough Anna Jarvis would in later years try and get the holiday removed from the calendar as a protest of the holiday's commercialization. There's even a story that she went into a restaurant, ordered a Mother's Day salad and then dumped it on the floor in protest. I wonder if she left a tip!

FATHER'S DAY

Father's Day is celebrated about a month after Mother's Day almost as an after-thought, acknowledging a fact we all know as ... "Ladies First" ... and that Mothers are more important than Fathers, even though theoretically you can't be a mother without having a "father" to assist you in the process. Although these days there are some that would argue that fact with you.

Since the beginning of time it's always been known that women have all the power, but our society doesn't give them that message. Women are the stronger sex. Just because men can lift heavier things, or wield swords in battle and conquer countries, people may think that men are stronger, but basically, they did all those other "macho" things just to impress women!

So in 1910, a good two years after Mother's Day was established, a woman named Sonora Smart Dodd came up with the idea for Father's Day, and it's been celebrated ever since.

How ideas were spread in those days no one knows. There was no internet. Even if you had a good idea how did you get other people to go along with you on it? Did she ring everyone's doorbell in the United States and tell them that honoring fathers would be a good idea, and see if they agreed? Did anyone even own a doorbell in those days?

Like with Mother's Day, many questions arise about how to celebrate this holiday for various reasons:

1. If your father mistreated you as a child do you still celebrate Father's Day?

2. If that was the case, did he give you any notice first or just spring it on you?

3. Did he spend most of your childhood in a drunken stupor?

4. If he manhandled you, did he use one of the following?

   a. A belt

   b. A hanger

   c. A tire iron – if this was the case you probably are not even here reading this book!

5. And if he was mean to you as a child but you went on to build a seven figure company and became hugely successful despite all that, do you buy him an extravagant present he couldn't afford on his own as a way of getting even?

6. If your father left your family when you were young and you were raised mostly by your Mom and only saw your Dad occasionally, but are still in touch with him today, what do you buy him? Maybe you could buy him some occasional furniture?

7. What if your Dad made you wear his hand-me-downs. This would be especially bad if you were a girl. If that was the case you could buy

him something frilly like a lacy scarf or maybe a pair of pantyhose.

8. If your Dad is no longer with us, you can still write him a beautiful note telling him what a good Dad he was and how much you miss him. Some people believe that people on the other side can see those things. (Note: don't try sending a note up in the sky in a balloon! Not only won't it work, it'll probably poison some unsuspecting animal!)

9. You can also visit the cemetery where he resides and say a prayer, maybe share a beer, and leave some flowers.

A WHIMSICAL HISTORY OF FATHER S DAY

The first one was held in Grafton, West Virginia thanks to a woman named Grace Golden Clayton back in December of 1907.

The lady was mourning the loss of her father in something known as the Monongah Mining Disaster which occurred in a town coincidentally called Monongah. In that disaster 361 men were killed, 250 of them being fathers.

That left around one thousand fatherless children. This same woman suggested to her pastor that he honor all of those fathers with a special day, and he did, but the holiday did not catch on and wasn't celebrated again for several years.

It was said that Grace Clayton was a quiet woman and didn't even promote the event nor did anyone else, which may have explained why it didn't catch on. Marketing and promotion wasn't really a thing yet.

Then in May of 1909 a woman named Sonora Smart Dodd of Spokane, Washington was sitting in church listening to a Mother's Day sermon when she decided she wanted to suggest a day honoring her Dad, Willam Jackson Smart.

Her mother had died in childbirth and her Dad who had fought in the Civil War raised the infant and his other five children all by himself. His birthday had been June 5th so the following year she petitioned the powers that be to celebrate the day as a "Father's Day" in Spokane.

The mayor of Spokane agreed but said he needed more time so two weeks later on July 19th, 1910, the city of Spokane celebrated its first Father's Day.

At that first memorable celebration young women handed out red roses to their fathers during a church service, and large baskets of roses were passed around with attendees requested to pin on a rose in honor of their own fathers, red for the living and white for those who had passed on.

Sonora Smart Dodd took it even a step further by riding through the city in a horse-drawn carriage and delivering roses and small gifts to fathers who were homebound.

It took quite a while for Father's Day to be officially recognized by the government, but finally in 1924 President Calvin Coolidge said he supported it in order to bring fathers and their children closer and to impress on the fathers their obligation to their families.

Then in 1966 President Lyndon Johnson issued the first presidential proclamation honoring fathers, but it still took until 1972 when President Richard Nixon signed it into law making it a permanent holiday

Now go buy your father a nice gift and thank him for having you!

INTERESTING FACTS ABOUT FATHER S DAY

1. The idea of a Father's Day was not met with the enthusiasm that Mother's Day was because, as one man said, "Father's don't have the same sentimental appeal that mothers do."

2. These days Father's Day is celebrated in many countries of the world.

3. There are more than 70 million fathers in the United States alone, which makes it very difficult to get them all in one room. Unless of course you have a big house. Try and imagine telling your wife to prepare for company and she asks, "How many?" And you say, "70 million!" It could put a strain on the relationship.

4. In 1916, President Woodrow Wilson used the modern technology of the day, which involved radio waves, and pressed a button in Washington D.C. which unfurled a flag in Spokane in honor of Father's Day.

5. And in 1924, President Calvin Coolidge urged all state governments to officially adopt Father's Day, which today is always celebrated on the third Sunday of June. What we need to find out is how

do you become President of the United States with a name like Calvin Coolidge? Have you ever met another person whose last name is Coolidge! It might just as well have been porridge!

6. Europe's version of Father's Day, along with South America is called St. Joseph's Day and is a traditional Catholic holiday that falls on March 19. Fathers of other religions get to be ignored that day. Just kidding!

7. It took the holiday quite a while to catch on with men though because many men looked at the supposed holiday as being "unmanly" with flowers and gift-giving, and were also against the commercialism of the holiday. Many of them resenting that they wound up paying for their own gifts.

8. There was actually a movement during the 1920's and 1930's to get rid of the separate Mother's and Father's Days and have one day called "Parents' Day" that would celebrate both parents at the same time.

9. But then The Great Depression hit the country and retailers pressed hard for a holiday they felt would be like a second Christmas for Dads promoting items like socks, ties, hats, smoking

accoutrements, golf clubs and other sporting equipment.

10. World War 2 solidified the holiday as a national institution and it was described as a way to honor our troops and to support the war effort.

11. As for commercialism, the holiday supposedly brings in more than 1 billion dollars spent on gifts!

INDEPENDENCE DAY

Independence Day is not just a movie starring Will Smith, it's the day in the United States that commemorates the signing of The Declaration of Independence on July 4, 1776. It's our main national holiday!

It's usually celebrated with barbecues, parades, picnics, outdoor events, sporting events, concerts and particularly fireworks for reasons unbeknownst to most people.

However, just between you and I, the reason was that one of the Founding Fathers, John Adams, wrote a letter to his wife on July 3, 1776 stating that (as per an article in the Huffington Post), "I am apt to believe that Independence Day will be celebrated by future generations as the great anniversary festival. It ought to be commemorated as the Day of Deliverance by solemn acts of Devotion to God Almighty. It ought to be solemnized with Pomp and Parade, with Shews,

Games, Sports, Guns, Bells, Whistles, Bonfires, and Illuminations from one end of this Continent to the other from this Time forward forever more."

Why some of those words were capitalized only John Adams would know, but this is how it was quoted in the article. And I'm guessing that years later it inspired the great Ed Sullivan to welcome people to his "shew". "A really big shew" as he would say. And if you're not old enough to remember Ed Sullivan please feel free to Google him!

A WHIMSICAL HISTORY OF INDEPENDENCE DAY

On July 4, 1776 the Continental Congress declared that the original 13 American colonies were free and independent and no longer were ruled by Great Britain, which more accurately should have been called "Not So Great Britain!" By the way, little known fact that England, Great Britain, and The United Kingdom are three separate entities.

In actuality the Congress voted to declare independence two days before, but didn't tell anyone because they had a feeling that around 150 years in the future people would prefer celebrating on July 4th. And they were right! The Fourth of July sounds so much better than "The Second of July!"

Meanwhile, the Revolutionary War was still going on and lasted from 1775 until 1783. That's the war during which George Washington set a very bad example for generations to come by standing up in a boat while crossing the Delaware River. He blamed it on tight pants, but that could just be a rumor.

The people in the colonies were tired of paying exorbitant taxes, which led to protests against "taxation without representation", boycotts and finally the Boston Tea Party during which the English closed down the Boston Harbor in retaliation for a group called "The Sons of Liberty" having destroyed an entire shipment of tea by dumping it into the water. If the water had been hot it would have been the biggest cup of tea the world had ever seen!

Originally it was thought that they had just spilled one or two cups of tea, which would not have been as big of a deal, but when they found out they had destroyed an entire shipment of tea, that was too much for the British who as everyone knows are very fond of their tea! To this day they are constantly taking tea breaks during the course of the day.

In response to the Declaration of Independence a British general named Sir William Howe launched an attack and captured New York City, thinking incorrectly that they could take advantage of the sales at Bloomingdales, but that didn't happen.

And then in 1778, a miracle happened. France joined the United States in its fight against the British, and actually fought. They didn't immediately surrender as they were known to do in later years.

The British finally gave in in 1783 and signed the Treaty of Paris in which Great Britain granted the United States its freedom, and Betsy Ross immediately began working on the flag.

Some say the British lost the war due to the fact that they had musicians leading them into battle. There was a fife, drum and bugle corps on every battlefield and anyone with any common sense knows that you can't sneak up on anyone while you're drumming loudly and playing a bugle.

"I HOPE THEY PLAY THAT ONE FROM YESTERDAY!"

After the first few battles the Americans were yelling out requests and threatening to hold a dance.

When the first Independence Day was celebrated in Philadelphia on July 4, 1777, in addition to the crude fireworks display, they also shot off guns and cannons, until people realized that was not such a great idea and limited the "illuminations" strictly to fireworks, which had been invented thousands of years before in China. The intent was to draw more people to the celebrations by making it look more interesting. For some reason people seem to be drawn towards fireworks.

QUESTIONS TO ASK YOURSELF DURING INDEPENDENCE DAY

This particular holiday seems to engender more questions than other holidays:

1. What am I going to do this summer?

2. How do I look in a bathing suit?

3. How am I going to lose at least 25 pounds in a week?

4. How do I get my hands on some cool fireworks when many states made them illegal?

5. How do I make friends with the Grucci family? (Known as America's "First Family of Fireworks" as a title of distinction.)

6. Do I have enough friends to invite them over for a barbecue?

7. Do I even have a backyard where I could have a barbecue?

8. In the event the answer to these last two questions is yes, do I own a barbecue grill with which to prepare the food?

9. If not why am I driving myself crazy?

10. How would I look in a three-cornered hat?

11. If the answer is "handsome" where would I even buy a three-cornered hat?

12. If I know any people of American Indian descent would it be uncomfortable for them to be invited to my barbecue, or should I just wait till Thanksgiving?

13. Will anyone ever be kind enough to make ear plugs for animals who don't know that fireworks are for celebrations and might be affected by them? If anyone does ever invent earplugs for animals, will someone be smart enough to figure out how to get the animals to use them?

INTERESTING FACTS ABOUT INDEPENDENCE DAY

1. The stars on the original American flag were arranged in a circle so that all the Colonies would appear equal.

2. July 8th, 1776, the first time that Independence Day was celebrated in Philadelphia was also the first day that the Declaration of Independence was read in public after people were summoned by the ringing of the Liberty Bell.

3. The White House held its first Independence Day party on July 4, 1801 during the administration of Thomas Jefferson.

4. Benjamin Franklin proposed using the turkey as the national bird, but the bald eagle which was eventually chosen, was the choice of John Adams and Thomas Jefferson.

5. The Declaration of Independence was signed by 56 men from the 13 colonies, who ranged in age from 27 to 70. The 70-year-old was Benjamin Franklin. The lead author, Thomas Jefferson, was only 33, often considered a magical number.

6. Only John Hancock signed the Declaration of Independence on July 4th. The other men all signed later.

7. In the weirdest of coincidences presidents John Adams, Thomas Jefferson and James Monroe all died on July 4th, and John Adams and Thomas Jefferson died within hours of each other on the same day July 4, 1826, the 50th anniversary of the signing of the Declaration of Independence. Adams was 90 and Jefferson was 83.

8. Every year on July 4th the Liberty Bell in Philadelphia is tapped, not rung, 13 times in honor of the original 13 colonies.

9. Congress made Independence Day an official paid federal holiday in 1938. Before that it was an unpaid holiday for federal employees.

10. In 1776 the population of the new nation was 2.5 million. Today as of 2017, it is 325.7 million.

LABOR DAY

Contrary to the way it sounds, this holiday is not about giving birth! It's a public holiday celebrated on the first Monday of September, honoring the American labor movement and what it's done for this country. To me it's the saddest holiday of all because it means the summer's over.

Even as a kid it would be sad. As soon as I saw Jerry Lewis on TV with his annual Labor Day Muscular

Dystrophy telethon, that signaled the end of summer and time to get ready to go back to school.

Personally, Labor Day makes me sad. First of all, it's one of the worst times to travel because the entire world is on the road and traffic is horrific. I can recall a time when some cars had no air conditioning, and you had to depend on the air rushing in from the highway as you sped along with the windows open. But that doesn't work when you're stuck in stopped dead traffic.

That all being said, there are questions that need to be answered about Labor Day.

How do you celebrate if you're unemployed, and basically have no labor?

What if you get to your camping spot and find that it's so crowded that you have to share your tent with a family of bears?

Labor Day is usually celebrated with a cookout, which is another word for a barbecue. What if your husband doesn't look good in a chef's hat and apron? Then what do you do?

What if you prepare tons of hamburgers, hot dogs and steaks - which is what most people prepare - and find out that all of your guests are vegan?

A WHIMSICAL HISTORY OF LABOR DAY

Labor Day pays tribute to the achievements and contributions to society of our American working force, the men and women who make this country what it is.

In the late 1800's conditions were very bad for our workers. Most worked seven days a week and 12 hours a day just to put food on the table, which is one of the strangest expressions in modern history. Where else would you put the food, ... under the table?

It was not uncommon for children as young as five or six to be working in factories, mills and mines across the country. There was obviously no height requirement for those jobs. How'd you like to drive a car built by a five year old?

Sanitary conditions were often non-existent, workers were often told to "try and hold it in", and safety conditions were as rare as work breaks.

Labor unions had first appeared during the late 18th century but became more powerful during the industrial revolution and began demanding better working conditions and better pay. To reach these ends they began organizing strikes and rallies, many of which turned violent, as in the Haymarket Riot of 1886.

In that riot that took place in Chicago, several policemen and rioters were killed. There were also reports of skinned knees and severe bruising. Most of the ones that were killed did not show up for work the next day, and were actually docked pay. That's how strict they were in those days.

In line with our love for parades, on Sept. 5, 1882, ten thousand workers took off from work to march from City Hall to Union Square, which I'm sure looked nothing like it does today. Things tend to change in 140 years.

But this line of 10,000 workers came to be known as the first Labor Day parade, which would always be celebrated on the first Monday in September.

It took Congress another 12 years before they made it a legal holiday because when it comes to politics, they moved as fast then as they do today!

And the only reason they finally did it was because of a huge labor strike that brought the worker's plight to the attention of the public. Before then it was considered a secret known to just about everyone!

It happened on May 11, 1894 when employees of the Pullman Palace Car Company went on strike in

Chicago to protest wage cuts and the firing of their union representatives.

On June 26th Eugene V. Debs who worked on the American Railroad Union and who was making so little money, he could only afford four letters in his last name, called for a boycott of all Pullman railway cars which crippled railroad traffic all across the country.

In response the government sent in troops to Chicago, resulting in even more riots during which twelve workers were killed. In those days they felt it was more effective to kill people by the dozen.

However, this resulted in the government giving in, in order to create peace with the workers. They finally passed a law that made Labor Day a legal holiday in the District of Columbia and the surrounding territories, which was great except that no one knew what that meant.

Several men lost sleep for four or five days trying to figure out where the surrounding territories were.

Interestingly enough, the true founder of Labor Day has never been identified. Some say it could have been the comedian Jerry Lewis who did his Labor Day telethon for so many years.

Others with more sense attribute the holiday either to Peter J. McGuire the co-founder of the American

Federation of Labor, or a different man with his own very similar name Matthew Maguire who just happened to be a secretary of the Central Labor Union, and who was known as the first secretary to refuse to wear sexy dresses to the office.

Either way, it was a man whose last name was pronounced the same way ... Maguire!

As I said earlier, to me it's the saddest holiday of the year because all it means is that the summer's over and it's back to school time.

INTERESTING FACTS ABOUT LABOR DAY

1. Oregon was the first state of the United States to make Labor Day an official public holiday, and that happened in 1887, once again probably before many of you were born. Otakara is from Oregon, and she can vouch for that (Not that it happened before you were born, but that it's thanks to Oregon that we honor the end of summer!). It was proposed by the trade unionists as the labor movement grew and the people associated with it gained more influence.

2. It became an official federal holiday in 1894 thanks to President Grover Cleveland, and by that time 30 states celebrated Labor Day.

3. The first Labor Day parade was organized by the Knights of Labor and was held in New York City, which is famous for its parades. It's also famous for the number of parades it holds and the things they honor. But when you think about it, parades can be weird. A parade is basically a very long line of people walking in formation usually to honor someone or something and to show gratitude for that person or event. That is a very strange way to show someone you're grateful for them.

If a guy helps you carry heavy bags home from the store, of course, you're grateful. But do you throw him a parade? No, of course not. You throw him a few bucks. It would be awkward to throw a parade for everyone you were grateful to.

What if you had a flat tire and a guy came along and helped you fix it. You would be extremely grateful, but throwing him a parade would be overkill. A nice size tip would come in handy. No one wants a parade. Everyone wants money!

Can you picture this conversation? Some guy's wife says, "Hey honey can we go away this weekend like we planned?" And he says, "Sorry dear, I helped this guy fix his car last week and he's so grateful he's throwing me a parade. I can't leave. I'm in the lead float and it wouldn't be right."

4. Some say it was a man named P.J. McGuire, a VP of the American Federation of Labor who initially proposed the holiday to the Central Labor Union, during the Spring of 1882, as a general holiday for the laboring classes. He chose the first Monday in September as being kind of between the holidays of the Fourth of July and Thanksgiving, which were also public holidays.

5. In fashion circles it's considered a "faux pas" (look it up!) to wear white after Labor Day. Especially white shoes. I (Jeffrey) personally wear white all year round.

HALLOWEEN

✦✦✦✦

"I'M LEAVING WHEN THE SUGAR MONSTER SHOWS UP!"

Halloween falls on October 31st and may seem like just an excuse for adults to dress up in crazy costumes, and drink too much so it turns into "Hurlaween" instead of Halloween.

It's definitely an excuse for women to dress like sexy cats or sexy nurses, or anything sexy at all which they'd be afraid to do at any other time of the year. On Halloween, it's considered not only acceptable, but kind of mandatory.

What kind of Halloween would it be without the sexy librarian who lets her hair down while making out with a pumpkin?

Also known as All Hallows' Eve or All Saints' Eve, it's celebrated in several different countries but always on Oct. 31st. In those countries it begins the three-day observance of Allhallowtide, which is the time dedicated to remembering the dead, including saints which are referred to as "hallows."

Deciding what to wear is crucial, and some people begin planning weeks before. Some people make elaborate costumes. I once saw a couple come to a party dressed as an Italian meal ... chicken parmagiana and spaghetti!

Many cities have stores dedicated specifically for Halloween. In New York, there's a chain of stores called "Ricky's" which are hair and beauty shops known for their wild Halloween offerings.

A WHIMSICAL HISTORY OF HALLOWEEN

Halloween has its origins in ancient times going back 2,000 years to the ancient Celtic festival of Samhain. The Celts lived in the area that is now Ireland, northern France, and the U.K.

The Celts would light bonfires and wear costumes to ward off ghosts. I guess they were the original cosplay creators long before TV and movies were ever invented.

In those days the Celts celebrated their new year on November 1, and in the 8th century Pope Gregory III declared November 1 as the day to honor all saints, which they called All Saints' Day. All Saints' Day incorporated some of the traditions that had been celebrated in Samhain.

The evening before November 1 was called All Hallows' Eve, which eventually became what we know as Halloween. The significance of November 1 was that to them it marked the end of summer and the harvest, and the beginning of what was usually a very cruel winter that was often associated with death.

And we think we have it rough when most of us can just turn up the heat when we need it!

The Celts believed that on the night before the new year, the boundary between the worlds of the living and the dead became blurred, which may have been the inspiration for Robin Thicke's hit song "Blurred Lines" 1300 years later!

So on the night before Nov. 1st when they celebrated Samhain it was believed that the ghosts of the dead would revisit the earth causing havoc and damaging crops.

On the bright side, they also felt that the presence of these ghosts or spirits made it easier for the Celtic priests known as Druids to make predictions about the future, which they felt was very important in guiding them through the brutal winters.

To commemorate the event the Druids built huge sacrificial bonfires to make sacrifices of crops and animals to their gods. Why they would waste crops by burning them when they were afraid of crop shortages is a question for the ages. And perhaps that's why you don't run into any Druids these days.

Fact is, they were banned in the 1st century by Roman emperor Tiberius and were gone by the 2nd century. And that's what you get for burning crops!

During the Samhain celebration, the Celts wore costumes consisting of animals' heads and skins, and were big into trying to tell each other's fortunes.

By the year 43 A.D. most of the previous Celtic territory had been conquered by the Romans who ruled those lands for 400 years and had their own ways of celebrating the new year.

They had two different festivals that were combined with Samhain. One was Feralia, a day in late October when the Romans would commemorate the passing of the dead, and the second festival was in honor of Pomona, the Roman goddess of fruit and trees.

The symbol of Pomona is an apple, which historians feel was what led to the Halloween tradition of "bobbing for apples."

When the colonists settled in what was to become America the European immigrants brought their Halloween customs with them. but because of the strict Protestant belief of the New England colonies the celebration of Halloween was very limited.

Not so in Maryland and the Southern colonies which were some of our first "partiers" and who carry on that tradition to this day. Everyone knows that Southern people love to party and have fun!

The holiday became more Americanized as it combined traditions from the many different European ethnic groups that came, as well as the influence of the American Indian tribes.

The earliest celebrations in America included parties celebrating the harvest, sharing scary ghost stories, fortune telling, singing, dancing, drinking to excess, and general mayhem.

By the mid-1800's the annual festivities were common but still not celebrated everywhere in the country. However, in the second half of that century there was a tremendous influx of new immigrants, especially millions from Ireland who were fleeing the great potato famine of 1846, and they helped to popularize the holiday in this country.

That's when people started going house to house asking for food or money, and that eventually became what we know as "Trick or Treating."

It was a common belief amongst young women that on Halloween they could predict the name or appearance of a future husband by doing tricks with yarn, mirrors or even apple parings. That must have led to some interesting match-ups! Where was Tinder when you needed it?

By the turn of the 19th century parties for children and adults became the most common way to celebrate Halloween, and by the turn of the 20th century, most of the religious and superstitious overtones of the holiday were lost by society's choice.

Due to widespread vandalism during the holiday many communities cracked down on Halloween celebrations, and by the 1950's it had become mostly a children's holiday. Trick or treating became a way for an entire community to celebrate together through their children while avoiding "tricks" by handing out "treats!"

QUESTIONS TO ASK YOURSELF AT HALLOWEEN TIME

1. Am I too old to go trick-or-treating?

2. If I decide to go, what kind of costume will I wear?

3. If I'm successful what will I do with all the candy?

4. If I offer it to other kids will I get arrested as a child molester?

5. Where do I find out how to carve a pumpkin?

6. Once I find that out, where do I even get a pumpkin?

7. If I happen to cut myself while carving that pumpkin do I leave some of the blood to make the pumpkin scarier, or do I go and get stitches right away?

8. If I live on a high floor in a tall apartment building and I put my pumpkin in the window, how do I get people to see it?

9. What if my pumpkin is scared of heights?

10. Do I have to move to an apartment on a lower floor just to let people see that I have a pumpkin?

INTERESTING FACTS ABOUT HALLOWEEN

1. Many Halloween traditions seem to have originated from Celtic harvest festivals that may have had pagan roots, but some people believe it actually started as a Christian holiday.

2. Pumpkins and Jack-O-Lanterns are two different things. A pumpkin only becomes a Jack-O-Lantern when you carve it into one. Their purpose is to frighten evil spirits.

3. In many countries where Halloween is celebrated, they light candles on the graves of the dead.

4. The word "Halloween" itself means "hallowed" or "holy evening." The "een" part comes from Scottish and is a contraction of the Scottish word "even" which became "e'en" and then finally became just "een" added on to the word Hallow.

5. The Anglican colonists in the southern part of the United States and Catholic colonists in Maryland recognized All Hallows' Eve in their Church calendars, but the holiday was strongly opposed by the Puritans in New England. They never had any fun!

6. It wasn't until the beginning of the 20th century

that it was celebrated in this country from coast to coast, and it was thanks to Irish and Scottish immigrants who popularized it during the 19th century that it finally caught on. So, the next time you dress up in something sexy or party your butt off on Halloween, you know who to be grateful for!

THANKSGIVING

In the United States, we are so prosperous that we need a holiday to remind us to be grateful. That holiday is called Thanksgiving. We are doing so well compared to other countries in the world that in some cities our slums are nicer than so called upscale neighborhoods in other countries.

It's a national holiday that is celebrated not only in the US, but also in Canada, some of the Caribbean islands, and Liberia of all places. Similar holidays are celebrated both in Germany and Japan.

One of the very first, if not the first Thanksgiving celebrations was said to have taken place in 1621 between the Plymouth colonists and the Wampanoag Indians, in what is now Massachusetts. It was prompted by a better than expected harvest.

Originally, they thought they'd all have to share one ear of corn, but miraculously it worked out that every person had their own ear of corn. The hardest part was trying to explain to the Indians why they called it an "ear of corn." Several of the Indians got confused, thought they were calling it "ear corn" and tried to insert it into their ears.

That first feast went on for three whole days, and if anyone had thought to bring music, there would have been wild dancing, because the Pilgrims were known to be great dancers. The only problem was that electricity hadn't been invented yet so they had to resort to humming ancient melodies, which did not elicit the same excitement. Hence no dancing occurred.

In modern times we associate the holiday with a huge turkey dinner along with stuffing, cranberry sauce, and sweet potatoes, which for some reason, some people insist on calling yams. Two different things entirely!).

At the original feast, there was little turkey, if any. They think most of the meat would have been venison, which was the popular meat of the time, and it was donated by an unlucky group of local deer. And definitely no potatoes because they weren't being grown yet in that area.

The practice of holding an annual feast of thanks for the harvest did not become a regular event until the late 1660's, when feasts became very popular for anyone who had not already starved to death.

George Washington, our first President was credited with proclaiming the very first nationwide Thanksgiving celebration, making Nov. 26, 1789 the special day, and proclaiming it "a day of public thanksgiving and prayer, to be observed by acknowledging with grateful hearts the many and significant favours of Almighty God." That was quite a quote!

In the beginning, there was some confusion about whether it was to be treated as a holiday celebration or as a religious service.

President Abraham Lincoln proclaimed the date of the holiday to be the final Thursday in November and made sure to do this before he was killed by John Wilkes Booth. It was thought that he did this to attempt to foster a sense of American unity between the North and the South, but because of the Civil War still going on, a nationwide date was not established until reconstruction was finished during the 1870's.

It wasn't until December 26, 1941 that President Franklin D. Roosevelt signed a joint resolution of Congress changing the date of the holiday from the last Thursday in November to the fourth Thursday in

November, I guess just in case one November wound up with five Thursdays. I have no time to check and see if that's even possible, but I'm guessing it is!

A WHIMSICAL HISTORY OF THANKSGIVING

The Pilgrims, as they came to be known, left Plymouth, England in Sept. of 1620 in a ship called The Mayflower, with 102 passengers who wanted to come to the New World as it was called, to freely practice whatever religion they wanted.

The crossing lasted 66 days, during which time they made plans to come down with scurvy, as many of them did during their first brutal winter on these shores.

As a matter of fact, most of them stayed on the boat during that first winter because the accommodations were better than they could find on land. The Indians had not thought to build any hotels, or bathrooms with indoor plumbing.

When they finally reached "The New Land" they wound up way far away from their intended destination, which would have been at the mouth of the Hudson River. Why some people think a river has a mouth has never been fully understood, but they wound up landing at a huge rock they called Plymouth Rock, named after the town they came from.

For three or four days they tried living on that rock but were unable to figure out how to do it, so they decided to build a village they called Plymouth as well because the Pilgrims were incredibly creative.

Aside from venison they wound up subsisting on seals, swans, and, believe it or not, lobster. I always wondered who the first man was to look at something as disgusting looking as a lobster and think to himself, "Man that would be good to eat!"

Only half of the original 102 passengers survived that first winter. And the ones that survived wished they hadn't.

There were three main Indian tribes in those days, the Abenaki tribe, the Pawtuxet tribe, and the Wampanoag tribe, and the most helpful of the Indians was named

Squanto from the Pawtuxet tribe.

Squanto taught the Pilgrims how to grow corn, extract sap from maple trees which they later taught to Canadians, how to catch fish, and how to avoid poisonous plants. In return the Pilgrims tried to steal everything they could from each of the tribes.

That first feast that went on for three days was organized by Governor William Bradford, the first Governor of the New World, who probably ran unopposed, since most of the other people were near death.

It was he who decided to invite the Indians, and boy was it a good thing he did. They brought all the good food. The Pilgrims had been eating wood. The only problem was they had no ovens or sugar so there were no desserts, which made the Indians sad as they were looking forward to having some cake.

Despite the success of that first Thanksgiving dinner in 1621, the next one didn't happen until 1623 due to a long drought that almost destroyed the whole previous year's harvest.

Two hundred years later, in 1827, the woman who wrote the nursery rhyme "Mary Had A Little Lamb", a writer and magazine editor named Sarah Josepha Hale, launched a campaign to establish Thanksgiving as a national holiday, and they agreed on the promise that she would stop creating nursery rhymes.

She kept her promise for 36 years during which time she lobbied every politician she could and finally in 1863, during the height of The Civil War, which was anything BUT civil, Abraham Lincoln proclaimed it a national holiday to be celebrated the last Thursday in November.

It stayed on that date for 76 years until 1939, when President Franklin D. Roosevelt moved it up one week, for some reason thinking it might help sales during The Great Depression.

Nobody liked that plan, especially people in The Great Depression. They felt even more depressed. So in 1941 he finally gave in and moved it back to the 4th Thursday in November and everyone lived happily ever after.

There is one story we can't forget to mention, and that is the historian who said that there have been other ceremonies of thanks among European settlers in North American well before the Pilgrims got there.

He uses the example of the Spanish explorer Pedro Menendez de Avile who in 1565 invited members of the local Timucua tribe to a dinner in St. Augustine, Florida, but the joke was on him because they got there too late to take advantage of the early bird special. It wound up costing him a fortune. Rumor has it that he didn't even leave a tip!

1. What do I have to be grateful for? This is a great way to make yourself feel happy by making a "gratitude list" of all the things you can be grateful for, including good health, the ability to use all of your senses, your family, children, a good job, a roof over your head, food to eat, and even personality traits like if you are a kind or a generous person. Those are all things you can be grateful for.

2. Have I ever actually met a Pilgrim, and if not do they in fact still exist?

3. Do I have any Pilgrims or potential Pilgrims in my family?

4. How would I look in one of those Pilgrim hats, and shoes with the big buckles? Do you feel like you could pull off that style? And where did that style go?

5. If the Pilgrims actually managed to trick the Indians into selling them Manhattan for only $24.00, how come they didn't go into real estate?

6. How did cranberry sauce get involved and is it a real thing?

7. If I have people over for dinner how do I get them to leave at a reasonable hour?

8. Do I try and figure out if I can save any of the leftovers until Christmas and serve them for dinner?

9. How will I survive family visits with people I have absolutely nothing in common with except that we share DNA?

10. How do I get through a big Thanksgiving dinner if I am hungry, I'm a vegan and all I can eat is the cranberry sauce, if it even exists?

11. Can I still feel grateful after sitting in traffic for three hours in what should be a 45 minute trip, to get to my grandmother's house where I will make meaningless small talk with people I hate for another three hours?

INTERESTING FACTS ABOUT THANKSGIVING

1. In parts of Australia, Thanksgiving is celebrated on the last Wednesday of November and was brought to the area by visiting American whaling ships. Some say they have never forgiven us for that.

2. On the island of Grenada in the Caribbean, they have a national holiday called "Thanksgiving Day," but it's not for the same reason. It commemorates the U.S-led invasion of the island in 1983 in response to the execution of the socialist Prime Minister Maurice Bishop by people in his own party.

3. In the Netherlands, they celebrate a Thanksgiving Day on the same day they celebrate it in America, but also not for the same reason. It's because many of the original Pilgrims who migrated to the Plymouth Plantation lived for a while in the city of Leiden, in the Dutch province of South Holland, and they were treated so well by the inhabitants, believe it or not, the holiday commemorates the hospitality they received. And that's the truth!

CHANUKAH

✡ ✡ ✡ ✡

"WHO KNEW RUDOLPH WAS JEWISH!"

This is a truly religious holiday as opposed to just a happy one, and it helps a lot if you can make the "Ch" sound with your throat in order to say it properly. Jewish people seem to be born with that ability. Either that or we just have a lot of phlegm. A friend of mine had an uncle who lived in Israel whose name was Chhhhhhhhh Chuchhhhhhh! See if you can pronounce that!

People who are "Chuchically" challenged are welcome to spell it Hanukkah, which then gives you the opportunity to just say it with a plain "H" as Hanukkah.

Chanukah is known as "The Festival of Lights" and has nothing to do with lightbulbs, although some Menorahs (candelabras for anyone not in the tribe) actually use tiny lightbulbs instead of candles. But that was not so back in the day when Moses was around because lightbulbs hadn't been invented yet. Electricity wasn't even discovered! That would be much later, thanks to Ben Franklin and his kite!

But I digress! Back to Chanukah. As the story goes, and I (Jeffrey) write this as a Jewish person so I take some liberty with the facts.

Chanukah is an eight-day holiday, the name of which means "dedication" in Hebrew, that has to try and compete with the popularity of Christmas.

Christmas is actually celebrated for 12 days, but most children get all their gifts on Christmas morning which makes it feel like a one-day holiday.

The closest we could come to matching that was by having a holiday lasting for eight days, signifying an ancient Biblical miracle involving what seemed to be only one day's worth of lamp oil lasting a full eight days.

126

That fact allows Jewish children to receive gifts on eight nights, instead of getting up early to find all of their gifts at the same time under a brightly colored fun-looking tree.

Instead of a tree, some Jewish people get what they refer to as a "Chanukah bush" and decorate it with Jewish symbols, then put the children's gifts under the bush.

How all this winds up involving a "dreidel", which is like a spinning square top that children play with during this holiday to win candy, pennies, or small toys, I have no idea, but I guess it's similar to using a rabbit and colored eggs to celebrate Easter.

Traditional food prepared for a Chanukah meal includes potato latkes which are like potato pancakes often eaten with apple sauce, which I'm sure they didn't even have in those days.

A WHIMSICAL HISTORY OF CHANUKAH

The holiday itself dates back to two centuries before Christianity, or about 2500 years ago, which again was before most of us were born, and its celebrated either in November or December because for some reason the Jewish holidays fall on different dates every year, as opposed to Christmas which is always on December 25th. That's why Jewish people can never make plans in advance. We don't know when our holidays will fall!

Theoretically it's supposed to fall on the 25th day of the Jewish month of Kislev, but since nobody knows when that is, it falls on a different day each year. If any of you knows when Kislev is please send me an e-mail.

The word Chanukah itself means "rededication" and celebrates what Jewish people refer to as a true miracle.

As usual in our history, someone wanted to enslave us. This time it was in Syria - big surprise - when the holy land was ruled by Greeks, and King Antiochus, which is another name you don't hear a lot, decided to try and make the Jews bow down to worship Greek gods. He even built a tremendous statue of a Greek god named Zeus in the Jewish temple, and sacrificed pigs in there.

I guess there was only one big Temple in those days, but the Ten Commandments instruct Jews to NEVER bow down, and to only worship the one true God and never worship idols. So they politely refused.

The Greeks recognized The Torah, or the Jewish holy book as a book of wisdom but not as a religious text and they tried to outlaw Judaism and The Torah. But the Jews were stubborn, and still refused to bow down to the Greek statues.

I guess the king got insulted by this and was in a very bad mood. A small group of Jews who called themselves "The Maccabees", which was probably the first and last all-Jewish street gang there ever was, were led by a man named Judah (The Hammer) Maccabee, who reportedly was nowhere near as funny as Judah Friedlander, but could probably take Conor McGregor in a fight.

He was the son of a Jewish priest named Mattathias the Hasmonean (which would be a great name for the lead singer in a band), and he decided to rebel and waged a three-year war against the Syrians, during which time his group recaptured Jerusalem from the Syrians, but unfortunately the Temple was destroyed in the process.

Jewish men are not known for being particularly handy, but in those days things were different, and they worked very hard to rebuild the Temple which became known as The Second Temple. Even before Neil Simon, we were always very creative people!

When they were finished building, they rededicated this Second Temple to God by lighting a lamp, known as the Menorah, which was a symbol of God's presence, and was supposed to stay lit day and night.

In those days the Menorah was a gold candelabrum with seven branches which represented knowledge and creation.

Oil was kept in barrels, and used as fuel for light in those days. The Greeks had sabotaged or "defiled" their oil, which was a word they liked to use back then.

But the Jews discovered one barrel that had not been touched, and even though theoretically they only had enough oil to keep the Menorah lit for just one night, miraculously the oil lasted for eight nights, which they thought was enough of a reason to start a holiday celebrated for eight days.

What happened after those initial eight nights no one seems to know. Maybe they got more oil, or maybe they just resigned themselves to being in the dark, but that's why the Menorah now has a place for eight candles with a ninth one on top called "the Shammos" that's used to light all the others.

The candles are placed in the Menorah one each night starting from right to left the way Hebrew is written and read, but they're lit from left to right, because the tradition is that you honor the newer thing first.

Chanukah is a very happy holiday!

QUESTIONS TO ASK ON CHANUKAH

1. Do I have a Menorah, and if so where is it?

2. Where do I get those tiny candles?

3. Do I still remember how to read Hebrew?

4. Is this the holiday where I have to eat matzoh or is that Passover?

5. Could I explain the difference?

6. Why is Chanukah called "the holiday of lights," and if we lose our electricity can we still celebrate it?

7. Can I get drunk on kosher wine?

8. Do I have the manual dexterity to spin a dreidel?

9. Do you think that dreidel spinning will ever make it to the Olympics, and if so will it be a winter or summer sport?

10. And if the sport catches on, will there be a special uniform for dreidel spinning?

INTERESTING FACTS ABOUT CHANUKAH

1. The significance of the oil makes it traditional to eat fried foods on this holiday, hence the prevalence of potato "latkes." They also favor brisket and a deliciously sweet dish made from carrots with brown sugar, sweet potatoes and cinnamon called carrot tsimmes! (Pronounced tzimmis. Try saying that three times fast!).

2. Gift giving was not part of the original tradition, but it has been incorporated into the holiday so that Jewish children don't feel badly when their non-Jewish friends get lots of gifts for Christmas.

3. The dreidel is like a square top that you spin that has four Hebrew letters on it, pronounced "Nun" (not like as in Priest, and rhymes with no other English word), Gimmel, Hei (pronounced "hay"), and Shin, which together stand for the Hebrew phrase "Nes Gadol Havah Sham" meaning "a great miracle happened here," referring to the oil lasting eight days.

4. To the children playing dreidel to see if they win candy or pennies, each letter stands for something else. If it lands on Nun you get none, Gimmel you get all, Hei you get half of the pot, and Shin you have to add one thing to the pot.

5. The game got started when Torah study was outlawed, but gambling was legal, so to hide the fact that they were studying they came up with this game to conceal their activity.

6. You won't even find the story of Chanukah in the Torah because all of the history I already explained happened *after* the Torah was written. If you've ever seen a Torah, you know that it's written on scrolls that you unroll as you read it, which makes it impossible to read on the subway, and there's literally no room to add anything. Not one bit of space is left!

7. Interestingly enough the holiday is mentioned in the New Testament in a story where Jesus, who was basically the star of that book, attended a feast referred to as "The Feast of Dedication." Most of the people who read that book have a hard time with the "Ch" sound!

CHRISTMAS

"I DON'T THINK WE CAN GET HIM OFF THE GROUND!"

Christmas is possibly the biggest holiday in the world celebrated by literally billions of people, and it's been a legal holiday in the United States since 1870.

The purpose of the holiday is to commemorate the birth of Jesus Christ, a simple man who started out as Jewish two thousand years ago, and wound up with his own religion. Whether he ever knew that or not is a matter of conjecture, but literally millions, and maybe billions of people are wearing his likeness around their necks.

It's celebrated every year on December 25th when people hope for snow so they can have a "white Christmas", meanwhile Jesus was born in a very hot climate where it probably has never snowed to this day. Just one of the many mysteries of the holiday of Christmas.

Jesus was born to a couple named Mary and Joseph in what is described in the Bible as an "immaculate conception." He was born in a manger, like a barn, because there was no room at the inn in the town of Bethlehem.

Bethlehem must have been a very popular destination in those days for them not to have had even one room, but it certainly adds to the story that Jesus was born in a stable, and visited by three wise men who came from the East, and who brought unusual gifts of gold, frankincense and myrrh.

The gold part was good, but no one knew what frankincense was. They confused it with Frankenstein, a monster that would be created two thousand years later and played by an actor named Boris Karloff, but that's a whole other story.

And some people claim to know what myrrh is, but no one is really sure. Anyway, these Three Kings as they came to be known, thought it was fitting to bring these kinds of gifts, and Mary and Joseph had no idea where to put them because the barn had no dresser, or closets, or any kind of storage space at all.

Christians believe that God came into the world in the

form of man to atone for the sins of humanity, of which there were many. When Jesus grew up he got his chance to atone for the sins of humanity, but it wasn't very comfortable as the Romans didn't treat him very well and wound up killing him by crucifying him, which is a terrible thing to do to anyone, much less the Son of God.

And it happened on a Friday which became known as Good Friday when it was anything but good for Jesus. He was treated very badly to say the least.

As the story goes after the crucifixion, the body was wrapped in a shroud, the Shroud of Turin, but according to Wikipedia, some people feel the body was stolen.

The religion teaches that three women went to the tomb and found the body gone, but three days later Jesus came back from the dead and was resurrected, which led to the creation of the holiday of Easter commemorating his resurrection. Not even David Blaine could do that!

After the resurrection Jesus was around preaching to his disciples for the next 40 days which is a magical number in the Bible, 40 days and nights, at which time he ascended to Heaven. Many people believe he will return some day as The Messiah. We sure could use some help!

EVEN MORE COOL STUFF ABOUT CHRISTMAS

1. The middle of winter, or the winter solstice as many refer to it, has long been a time of celebration for societies going back centuries before Christ. It was a time when the worst of the winter was behind them, and the promise of longer days and more hours of sunlight lay ahead.

2. Many people refer to Christmas as Yule or the Yuletide season. Yule was a holiday celebrated by the Norse, from December 21 through January. It was to recognize the return of the sun, and fathers and their sons would bring home huge logs, set them on fire and feast until the fire burnt out, which could take as long as 12 days, which by the way could possibly represent the 12 days of Christmas.

3. The term "The Norse" refers to anyone from a Scandinavian country. Like Iceland, Denmark, Norway or Sweden.

4. The Norse held the belief that each spark from the fire represented a new pig or calf that would be born in the year to come. That was important to them.

5. So Yule was basically a Pagan holiday which when Christianized became known as Christmastide, which may have something to do with the term "sending Christmas tidings." Because otherwise no one knows what the word "tidings" even means. When was the last time you used the word "tidings" in a sentence?

6. Food was generally scarce in most areas of Europe so this time was perfect for celebration because it was one of the only times of the year when food was plentiful. The reason was that most cattle were slaughtered during that time so as to save money on feeding them during the winter. It was a bad time to be cattle.

7. On the other hand, it was also the time of the year when most wine and beer were finally fermented, so most people were so high they didn't even realize they were killing all of their cattle.

8. Now in Rome however, they celebrated a different holiday at that time of year which they called Saturnalia. It was in honor of Saturn, the god of agriculture, which some say was the only culture they had.

9. Saturnalia began the week before the winter solstice and lasted for a whole month. It was a holiday of hedonism, where pleasure was the

emphasis, and it was also a time when the Roman social order was turned upside down, when - for that month - the slaves would become the masters, and peasants ran the city. That had to be interesting.

10. And just like today, schools and businesses would be closed, but I have a feeling they were very different kind of schools and businesses than we know today. In those days they had things like philosophy stores where people would come in and the owner would say, "To be, or not to be, what is your question?"

11. The Romans celebrated another holiday at that time called Juvenalia, which sounds like something that should probably be against the law, especially if they were to try and revive that today. It was a feast that honored the children of Rome. I would have definitely kept my kids home!

12. And, believe it or not, there was even a third holiday at that same time, but it was only celebrated by members of the upper classes, marked by those who bathed more than once a year. It was the celebration of the god Mithra, the god of the "unconquerable sun." And it fell on December 25th, the day we celebrate Christmas.

13. Mithra, which sounds an awful lot like the Japanese horror film Mothra, was supposedly an infant god who they believed was born of a rock. That made a lot of sense to those people at the time, and for some of those people was considered the most sacred day of the year. And why not?

14. In the earliest days of Christianity Jesus' birth was not even celebrated. It was Easter that was the main holiday. People in the Western part of the country wanted to call it Wester, but fortunately, the Easter people won out because Wester just sounds weird.

15. It wasn't until the 4th century when church officials finally decided to celebrate the birth of Jesus as a holiday, however some historians believe that Jesus was actually born in the Spring, questioning why shepherds would be herding in the middle of winter! Good question. Raise your hand if you have an answer!

16. It was Pope Julius 1 who chose December 25th as the date of Jesus' birth, which some say was an effort to get rid of the embarrassment of Saturnalia.

17. It started out being called "The Feast of the

Nativity" which spread to Egypt by the year 432, which by most was considered to be a good year, and it took another 150 years or so before it was adopted by England towards the end of the 6th century, a very enlightened time for many!

18. The celebration we know as Christmas finally got to Scandinavia by the end of the 8th century, because they wanted to get presents also, and this led to the invention of wrapping paper, which is used a lot today in stores all across the country like Bloomingdales, and Walmart.

19. Today in the Greek and Russian Orthodox churches the holiday of Christmas is celebrated 13 days after the 25th, which they also refer to as "The Epiphany" or "Three Kings Day," commemorating the day the three wise men finally showed up in the manger.

20. After Christianity mostly replaced Paganism by The Middle Ages, Christmas became the time of the year when the upper classes would entertain the lower classes in order to show their gratitude for their relative lives of comfort. I say "relative" because no one had toilets or showers yet!

21. It wasn't always easy for Christmas though and it was actually outlawed in the early 17th century in

Europe when a wave of religious reform took over the continent, and Oliver Cromwell and his Puritan forces who vowed to rid England of its decadence actually cancelled all Christmas celebrations in 1645.

22. It wasn't until Charles II was restored to the throne that the holiday of Christmas was also restored. I guess Charles I couldn't be bothered with that.

23. But the Pilgrims who came to America were even more conservative than Cromwell and hastily banned Christmas again. It was not celebrated in early America, and was actually outlawed in Boston from 1659 to 1681. You could wind up in the stockade or strapped to the dunking stool for wishing anyone a Merry Christmas in those days. If you even exhibited Christmas spirit and someone found out you could be fined five shillings, which in those days was enough to buy two Big Macs and a side of fries.

24. But for some reason in the Jamestown settlement, Christmas was celebrated and enjoyed by all who lived there, according to founder Captain John Smith, which was probably an alias. No one is really named John Smith! It's just used as an example of a typical American name in comedy!

25. Jamestown, by the way, was the first place that eggnog was consumed for the very first time!

26. After the American Revolution Christmas was looked at as an English custom and fell out of favor, which was why it wasn't declared a federal holiday for almost another hundred years, until 1870.

27. Christmas didn't really become popular in the U.S. until the 19th century when it was changed from a Mardi Gras-like celebration to a day of solemnity. A day of peace and nostalgia to be celebrated with one's family.

28. The lower classes of people would often riot during Christmas time due to high unemployment and in 1828 in response to a Christmas riot in New York City, the city's first police force was established. It was the earliest version of the NYPD.

29. Two writers, Washington Irving and Charles Dickens shaped the way Christmas is celebrated today, through their writings, Irving's "The Sketchbook of Geoffrey Crayon" and Dickens' "A Christmas Carol", where people of all classes celebrate together in harmony. The only time that harmony is lacking is when they try and sing

Christmas carols! But thanks to them the holiday stressed the importance of charity and good will towards all men.

30. And lastly, it was construction workers who started the tradition of transporting a huge Christmas tree to Rockefeller Center in New York City in 1931. It generally ties up traffic for days, but it's a beautiful sight to behold.

QUESTIONS TO ASK YOURSELF AT CHRISTMAS TIME

1. How far in advance do I have to start stressing out that the holiday is coming?

2. If Jesus was such a peaceful man, why is his holiday so stressful?

3. When is the best time to buy a tree and where do I go to get one?

4. If I can't find a tree will a bush do?

5. If I can't afford ornaments can I use cheese?

6. Do I have to buy gifts for EVERYONE?

7. Where am I supposed to get the money for all those gifts?

8. As long as I don't kill anybody, is it a sin to rob a bank in order to have money to buy all those gifts?

9. Will anyone be able to tell if I get boxes from expensive stores but buy my gifts at Walmart and put them in the fancy boxes?

10. If friends or relatives from out of town come to visit, how long do I have to let them stay before I can throw them out?

11. What if they try and stay long enough to have "squatters rights?"

12. Do I always leave an empty chair just in case Jesus actually does show up?

13. When my cat messes up the decorations on my tree that took hours to put on, do I have to call PETA to keep from killing it?

14. What does Santa Claus, the North Pole, and elves have to do with any of this?

INTERESTING FACTS ABOUT CHRISTMAS

1. The term "immaculate conception" actually refers to the birth of Jesus' mother Mary, not Jesus who was said to have had a "virgin birth", and that Mary was said to be "free from original sin."

2. Jesus was baptized by none other than "John the Baptist" which was a name he earned by baptizing people, often against their will. He would just sneak up on someone and before they knew what was happening he was baptizing them ... hence John the Baptist.

3. After being baptized, Jesus fasted for 40 days and nights in the Judean desert, which is how he stayed so thin, and developed great abs. During those 40 days the Devil tried to tempt him over and over again, which became known as "The Temptation of Christ", until he realized he was wasting his time, and finally gave up and Jesus returned to Galilee to begin his ministry.

4. As far as the Christmas tree is concerned, according to the Encyclopedia Britannica the use of evergreen trees, which I don't think you would ever find in the desert, was common to symbolize eternal life, and was used by ancient Egyptians, Chinese, and Hebrews.

5. Tree worship was also common among pagan Europeans, and in Scandinavia, they use decorated trees at the New Year to scare away the devil. I think it works because the devil has not been sighted around there for quite a while.

EPILOGUE

Well, you people have been an absolutely wonderful audience. Give yourselves a hand. We hope that nothing we wrote was offensive to anyone as it was all meant in jest and good fun, in the spirit of inclusivity and good humor.

We look at comedy as a "Healing Force" and if we can laugh at ourselves and then at each other it brings everyone together, and it makes the world a better place.

We also hope this guide has been helpful to you in navigating your way through the holidays without doing anything drastic or harming anyone, including yourself.

Happy Holidays to all of you, and remember to stay in touch! Visit Jeffrey at www.comedymatterstv.com and Otakara at www.otakaraklettke.com

Please let us and others know what you thought about this book and PLEASE **leave a review**! Without a steady stream of reviews, this book will get lost in the fast running waters of Amazon. That's how Amazon rates its books.

By leaving a review, you are helping others to know what to expect and also helping this book to be found. One minute of your time to do that will be appreciated more than we can say. We promise to read each and every one!

As our thanks for buying this book, we would love to give you a mini version of Jeffrey's hit book **Man Robs Bank With His Chin.**

Visit https://www.comedymatterstv.com/free/
for your FREE download!

Now go back to Page 1 and start reading all over again! And remember to tell your friends!

And a special shout-out to Wikipedia and History.com from which many of the facts stated in this book were taken.

ABOUT THE AUTHORS

Jeffrey Gurian

Jeffrey Gurian is a comedy writer, performer, director, author, producer, doctor and Healer. He's written material for comedy legends such as Rodney Dangerfield, Joan Rivers, George Wallace, Phil Hartman, Richard Belzer, and Andrew "Dice" Clay.

Jeffrey has performed stand-up at all the big clubs in NYC and L.A. and was featured several times on Comedy Central's hit Kroll Show with Nick Kroll,

John Mulaney, Amy Poehler, Seth Rogen, Laura Dern and Katy Perry. He was in the viral "Too Much Tuna" sketch, was the very first person to be pranked with "Too Much Tuna", and was also a regular on-air personality on Sirius XM's Bennington Show, where he brought on special guests/friends like Russell Peters, Trevor Noah, Colin Quinn, Artie Lange, Susie Essman and Lisa Lampanelli.

He writes a weekly column covering the comedy scene for The Interrobang called "Jumping Around With Jeffrey Gurian", and has also written for MTV, National Lampoon, Weekly World News and many Friars Roasts.

In 1999 he launched Comedy Matters, a celeb-based online entertainment column that has evolved into Comedy Matters TV, an internet TV channel with over 500 A-list celebrity interviews and well over 1.9 million views. He's produced shows starring Kevin Hart and Susie Essman, and according to Paul Provenza, and Nick Kroll is known by everyone in comedy.

This is his 6th book. His 5th book on Happiness, "Healing Your Heart, By Changing Your Mind- A Spiritual and Humorous Approach To Achieving Happiness" reached Best Seller status on Amazon. Visit his website at http://www.comedymatterstv.com

154

Otakara Klettke

USA-based international best-selling author Otakara Klettke is a former investigative TV reporter in her home country of the Czech Republic.

In 2016, her best-selling non-fiction book, *Hear Your Body Whisper: How to Unlock Your Self-Healing Mechanism* became an instant bestseller on Amazon and remained a bestseller for almost two years straight. Its Russian translation rights have recently been published in all Russian-speaking countries.

Inspired by her experience of homeschooling her daughter while raising five dogs, Otakara created the *Detective Bella Unleashed* series of middle-school detective thrillers written from a dog's point of view. The first book in the series, *The Case of Missing Max*, came out in 2017, the second, *The Case of False Blame*, in 2018.The books provide a hilarious combination of humor and mystery along with eye-opening insights into how dogs view their humans.

The success of her books, her knack for communicating to a broad audience, and her ability to break complicated subjects down into compelling yet easy-to-understand pieces, have earned Otakara dozens of interviews on podcasts such as Learn True Health, Discover Your Talent, and many radio shows, webinars, and workshops.

Otakara lives with her family and pets in Oregon. She quenches her thirst for curiosity by traveling, and learning from books and people.

To connect with Otakara visit her at
www.otakaraklettke.com

ABOUT THE ILLUSTRATOR

Alex has loved drawing since he could pick up a pencil, sketching through his school years, he was known for being the doodler in his class. Growing up he loved comic books and manga, particularly influenced by Akira Toriyama's 'Dragon Ball'.

At college he began taking an interest in animation and taking his drawing more seriously. This is the second book featuring Alex's illustrations, the first being the Children's book 'Detective Bella Unleashed - The Case of False Blame' by Otakara Klettke.

Alex is an irredeemable tea addict and enjoys wordplay and internet memes in his spare time - if he ever has any!

He lives and works in Derby, UK.

Made in the USA
Las Vegas, NV
08 February 2022

43496197R00095